Clever, but still—part of the enemy edifice, and as such, an apologist for evil

The Making Of A Mandarin

The Making Of A Mandarin

Antony Part

ANDRE DEUTSCH

First published 1990 by
André Deutsch Ltd
105-106 Great Russell Street
London WC1B 3LJ

British Library Cataloguing in Publication Data

Part. Sir, Anthony
The making of a mandarin
1. Great Britain. Civil Service. Biographies
I. Title
354.41006092

ISBN 0 233 98557 3

Printed in Great Britain by
St Edmundbury Press, Bury St Edmunds, Suffolk

Contents

Acknowledgements

I acknowledge with thanks permission from the Institute of Management Consultants to use material from my article in *Management Symposium 3*: 'Business and Government', and from the Institution of Structural Engineers to draw on my Maitland Lecture delivered at their invitation.

My thanks are also due to the librarians of the Department of Education and Science, the Property Services Agency and the Department of Trade and Industry for their help in supplying and checking information about several past events.

CHAPTER ONE

The Nature of a Mandarin

In its total effect, 'Yes, Minister' was about as much like real life in Whitehall as that other brilliant television show 'Are You Being Served?' was like real life in the retail trade. In recent times the media and some Ministers have done a good deal of sniping at the Civil Service, and this denigration has affected both morale and recruitment. The damage cannot be remedied by flattering annual messages that are not reflected in subsequent speeches and actions.

This book aims to reveal a different perspective. It shows that working for government is much more challenging and interesting – and no less full of humour – than anything normally portrayed by the media.

What does it take to make a mandarin? What kind of people are they? Are they, as they would like to appear, wise and well informed counsellors or are they men and women delighting in the privacy of the corridors of power and with a low opinion of Ministers and other politicians? Are they experienced realists with a good practical knowledge of the world outside Whitehall or, as they have been called, a monastic order remote from reality? Are they academics *manqués* (or *manquées*, as the case may be)? Do they faithfully serve the government of the day or do they regard themselves, as one commentator has suggested, as a separate estate of the realm? Are they good at getting things done as opposed to thinking and advising about them? In the modern world of rapid communications can they work with adequate speed? Are they insular by inclination and experience or can they operate effectively on the international stage?

Nearly all those who have spoken or written about Whitehall have never made a career in it, and there is a limit to what serving civil servants may publish.

My aim is to open some windows on the real Whitehall. I have done this not by using researchers or surveys or, as sometimes happens, by indulging in gossip dressed up as research, but by relying on personal experience over nearly forty years to illustrate the widening perspective from that of a new entrant to that of a Permanent Secretary and to discuss a variety of topical issues on the way. This approach requires, as a start, a sketch of the early influences which helped to shape the man.

In 1915 my father, Alexander Part, aged thirty nine, old Harrovian, Cambridge graduate, barrister-at-law, former 'devil' to F. E. Smith, later to become the first managing director of Trust Houses, and already involved with the Secret Service (which in later years he used as a cover for his marital infidelities) married my mother.

His family origins were in Lancashire. In the early nineteenth century his grandfather, Thomas Part, married Frances Woodcock, with whose family he was connected through the law firm of Woodcock & Part. Frances was able to claim direct descent through the female line from John of Gaunt, Duke of Lancaster. This connection was a matter of pride but no practical value to later generations.

Thomas built up a considerable reputation. His energy manifested itself in his childhood when his daily walk to school and back measured twelve miles. He became the leading legal expert in Lancashire on the development of railways and did much Parliamentary legal work in that connection. He was prominent in advising coal and iron companies and was one of the solicitors acting on behalf of Sir Robert Peel's government in the prosecutions in 1842 which followed the Chartist riots. He was also responsible for the spacious layout of the town of Southport, a new concept in town planning with broad tree-lined streets, open spaces, zoning of buildings for different purposes and the avoidance of terrace housing.

Having made his pile, Thomas, like many others before him, moved south to Hertfordshire, where his son Charles Thomas became High Sheriff of the county and a Master of Fox Hounds – and lost most of his financial inheritance through speculative share-dealing. As High Sheriff he received in the early nineties a letter from the solicitors to the Assize Judge. This said –

> Mr Justice Hawkins has not yet determined whether when he conducts the Assizes he will attend divine service. But should he do so, he would be glad if you would instruct the Vicar that the sermon should be very short and should not exceed three minutes.

An interesting side-effect, perhaps, of having an established Church.

My mother, Una Snowdon, was my father's second wife, his first – Ethel, a Welsh girl – having sadly died at no great age in 1912. One characteristic apart, the marriage of my mother and father was a marriage of opposites – right through to the fact that my mother's family came not from Lancashire but from Yorkshire. Unlike her husband Alick, Una – ten years the younger – was strikingly good looking, constant in her affections and high in her moral standards. She was also very musical and played the piano to a high amateur standard. She loved going to concerts at the Albert Hall, often by courtesy of a family who had three debenture tickets there. The origin of this rather unusual arrangement was that when the Albert Hall was being built debentures were offered to the public. Alfred, a young scion of the family, applied for two and reported this to his rather formidable mother.

'Is it your idea, Alfred, that you might use these tickets to take a young woman to these concerts?'

'Well, yes, Mama.'

'Alfred, you had better buy three debentures,' the third being, of course, for a chaperone.

The one characteristic that, unfortunately, my father and mother did share was a stubbornness, derived perhaps from their respective counties of origin, and a determination to wear the trousers. The seeds of the conflict which was to influence my life so strongly were sown on the day of their wartime wedding.

They both came of a robust generation, the robustness rooted in a strict family upbringing, comfortable housing, good food and an extensive knowledge of the Bible. They saw, I often think, more changes than any other generation. In 1876, when my father was born, there was no electricity and neither motor cars nor aircraft had been invented. Nor had telephones, radio, television, penicillin, or X-Rays. By the time that my father died in the mid-1950s, we had advanced (if that is the right word) to nuclear warfare, nuclear power and the exploration of space. And this generation had experienced two world wars of unparalleled destruction.

Women in the late nineteenth century had no cause to be experts in these technical phenomena. Unreality in matters outside normal domestic experience persisted for many years. My father's brother Dealtry lived in a handsome William and Mary house in the Bedfordshire countryside, surrounded by a quite extensive acreage. At the start of the Second World War one of the guests was woken early on a winter's morning by a maid who went to draw the curtains back. The guest was doubtful about this as the black-out was still in force. She put this point to the maid, who replied, 'Do you thing it matters, Madam? In our own grounds?' This unreality extended in many cases to matters such as banking. My father's mother was the originator of a remark which subsequently became famous. When she went into her local bank in St Albans one day, the manager asked if he could have a word with her. He said 'I am afraid I have to tell you, Mrs Part, that you are somewhat overdrawn.' My grandmother replied, 'Oh I'm so sorry; I'll write you a cheque at once.'

My father and mother's married life began in Cheyne Walk on the riverside in Chelsea, where they had some experience of Zeppelin raids. But after my younger sister Rosemary was born they moved to a much larger house in Ashburn Place, near Gloucester Road station. The structure of the house reflected the social structure of the mid-nineteenth century. A hundred stairs, attic at the top, then the servants' bedrooms, then the day and night nurseries, then the principal bedrooms, then the large drawing room with the splendid Steinway concert grand piano which my father gave my mother as a wedding present. Then, on the ground floor, the dining room with french windows opening on to the gardens. It was in this room, set up for a formal dinner for twelve that, as a small boy of perhaps four, I experienced my father's first attempt to interest me in the world of business. 'My boy,' he said, 'do you know that Mr Colman makes his money out of the mustard that people leave on their plates?' This gave me furiously to think. I could not work out how Mr Colman could get back this amount of mustard, in order somehow to make money out of it. A sign that I was not cut out for an early entry into commerce!

In the basement, conditions heavily underscored the difference between the social classes. The fifteen stairs down were shielded from the view of anyone in the hall and they were of bare stone. I have never forgotten the tears of a young maid who, carrying the tea tray down from the drawing room, stumbled at the top of the basement stairs and fell all the way down. At least my mother did not follow the fashion of those days and stop her wages until the cost of replacing the broken china had been covered.

The kitchen was large and high-ceilinged and got quite a bit of light through the 'area' window, but the bedrooms and other facilities were dank and dark and uncomfortably reminiscent of a Dickens novel. There was the usual hierarchy of servants: butler, cook, maid and, of course, nanny. These kinds of class consciousness and social contrast and many others of finer gradation were to lie at the heart of one of the most remarkable events in British political history – the rejection of Winston Churchill's bid to remain at the helm of government in 1945. At that stage his great wartime leadership weighed lightly in the scales against the determination, of returning servicemen in particular, that post-war Britain should be a fairer, less class-ridden country than before the war.

The early twenties were my father's heyday. He had a beautiful talented wife, four children, a large house, a car and chauffeur. As the first managing director of Trust Houses he was responsible for a considerable empire devoted to the cause of temperance and of improving the food and facilities in pubs and setting up a chain of such places around the country which would be guaranteed in advance to provide food, drink and accommodation at a predictably acceptable standard.

He had an interest in the new General Trading Company, a shop set up after the First World War for the benefit of his youngest brother, Alfred, an attractive bachelor, 'to keep him out of mischief' according to my father. It sold antique furniture, wedding presents and a variety of other gifts and quickly earned the patronage of members of the Royal Family and has prospered under three successive generations of Parts – for fifteen years under my father himself.

He also became chairman of the Colne Valley Water Company in Hertfordshire, one of the best managed privately-run water companies in Britain. It was on this company's writing paper that in the late 1940s he corresponded genially with Aneurin Bevan, as Minister of Health, whose recent letter had said how interesting the work of the company was. My father replied, 'I should have valued your expression of interest in my company even more highly had I not thought it comparable with the interest taken by the lion in the lamb.' His letters to his family were equally caustic, mostly in one sentence paragraphs. At the beginning of the year that my wife and I were to spend in America on a Harkness Fellowship in 1950–51 he wrote to her briskly, 'If you are going to allow yourself to be driven around the United States by Antony, you must prepare for Death.' Luckily his fears were not justified, though in the final month of that otherwise marvellous experience a knife thrust nearly killed the driver instead.

My mother was no less active than my father. In the early, happy, years of her marriage she became responsible for the furnishing and décor of many of the growing number of Trust Houses. She did welfare work in Camberwell (in those days it was known as 'going slumming') and in later years she stood, unsuccessfully, as the Conservative parliamentary candidate for that constituency. She had one very special achievement. In each of several years she wrote and produced a pantomime at the Chelsea Palace theatre across the Kings Road from the old Chelsea Town Hall. The songs were quite often popular songs

ILL?

of the day with different words, but when they were not she composed them. She also conducted the orchestra. She was wise enough to engage a professional actor to play the lead, but the other parts were played by her friends or their children. In one year the youngest member of the cast was eight years old and the oldest eighty. The eight year old made an unexpected and hugely popular entrance by tripping up behind the scenes and falling through a mock fire on to the stage centre back.

In 1924 I was sent to my preparatory school at Wellesley House, Broadstairs. In those days we nearly all went by train from Victoria and left behind a large number of young mothers, who took out their handkerchiefs to wave goodbye to their small sons and then dabbed their eyes as they turned round to leave the platform.

That year turned out to be a bad one for my father. He was forced to resign as managing director of Trust Houses because he was judged to have over-expanded the company and the year also marked his first major excursion outside the bounds of his second marriage. After that his business career never prospered to the same extent and his marriage headed towards divorce, a more serious step then than, perhaps unfortunately, it is today. Indeed, my father as what was then known as 'the guilty party' was gravely concerned lest all his friends should desert him. The decree absolute was issued on my fourteenth birthday. My mother came down to Harrow to tell me about it.

'Did you realise there was anything wrong between your father and me?' 'No,' I replied, for in that large house they had succeeded in keeping their quarrels from me. The news came as a considerable shock, but I had no idea on that distressing day (for I deeply loved my mother) that the shockwaves would last for a quarter of a century. A 'third party' was involved (though not in formal legal terms) in the shape of Edith Sharpe, an actress fairly well known, particularly in Shakespearian parts, whom he married not long afterwards.

Fourteen, I discovered, was a bad age to be at the time of one's parents' divorce. Not long before one had been regarding them as gods; all too soon they appeared as very fallible human beings.

I found myself having to judge between them, to appraise their respective calumnies (for feelings rose very high) and to negotiate such mundane matters as who should visit me at Harrow on which weekend. On one occasion they each picked peremptorily on the same Sunday and I had not the strength of mind to tell them of the conflict. I did, however, succeed in spacing them out (the first and second service, so to speak). The only happiness on that unhappy day was that I ate two teas at the school shop, each finishing with that most magnificent of all ice-cream concoctions – a Knickerbocker Glory. At Christmastime they each insisted, year after year, on having their big celebration on Christmas Day. Neither of them would shift to Boxing Day and in 1953 – twenty five years after the divorce – there was still so much tension between them that, in addition to lunch in one place and dinner in the other, my wife and I had to divide forces for tea.

All this gave rise to an instinct in me for conciliation which stayed with me throughout my working years. Various of my colleagues would probably say that this claim sits oddly with the after-effects of my wartime work as a part-time army interrogator of German prisoners-of-war in the field. They might also say that my determination to make a success of any activity in which I was engaged smacked too much, by way of push and hustle, of my experience of serving under General Montgomery in his campaigns in the Western Desert and in Normandy.

But for fifty years the successful working of teams of mixed skills (so essential to modern government and business) has ranked high among my objectives, and an ability to conciliate has had something to do with bringing co-operation about.

Meanwhile life at school was full of activity. My excellent prep school had some very good teachers, especially of the Classics. Work went well and a generous age allowance in the scholarship exam at Harrow enabled me to start there soon after my twelfth birthday. The régime was quite demanding. We were woken at 6.45 and Early School started at 7.30 with prayers led by one's form master. In my second year all of us facing the prospect of the School Certificate made our first acquaintance with our rather forbidding form and Classics master, C. G. (Cocky) Pope at just such an Early School. He strode into the room, where none of the boys was known to him, picked up the prayer card (which he alone had) and addressed his first words to his new class: 'We'll start with the General Confession. Speak up!' We had trouble in identifying the General Confession, let alone in speaking up.

After passing School Certificate in the following summer, I began to specialise in French and German for the remaining four years of my time at Harrow. This was balanced only by History, English and a little Latin. Mathematics stopped for me at the School Certificate and in the whole of my education at my prep school and Harrow science was completely missing, except for half a day's botany at Wellesley House. This was a nonsense with an increasingly technological world already in prospect. My own career turned out to involve spending many years working alongside various kinds of engineer and scientist as well as architects and quantity surveyors. A good supply of wet towels was needed to master enough of the technology to become an effective partner. Learning some of the elements at school would have been much more satisfactory.

Splendidly stimulating though my fifth- and sixth-form masters were, teaching their pupils a lot more than French and German, I think that in the external examinations at both sixteen and eighteen (by whatever names they may be called) one should be required to offer a balance between the arts and sciences. Lack of acquaintance with the arts is just as bad for a scientist as a similar lack of science is for an arts student. At undergraduate level, I am now inclined to think that a similar balance should be prescribed. It is increasingly recognised that an undergraduate's education should be regarded as only a step in a process that should continue – in one form or another – for many years.

At the moment the most clamant need in Britain is to get more science and technology into the picture. The vigorous expansion of technological education a quarter of a century ago was not continued for long enough or with sufficient intensity. Inspired teaching, which I received in generous measure, is rare. But it cannot be an adequate substitute for a lack of balance in preparing people for life in the modern world.

Not everyone at Harrow worked hard – or perhaps one should say worked to great effect. But most people played hard, especially in my house, Elmfield. In my time it bred some notable sportsmen. Prominent among them was Peter Studd. Tall, fair-haired and good looking, he was made to become a public figure and indeed interrupted his directorship of De la Rue to become Lord Mayor of London in 1970. During his term of office the Lord Mayor is allowed one substantial foreign trip. Peter chose the Far East and on his return I received a message at the DTI that he would like to tell me his impressions. Peter received me in the Lord Mayor's Parlour, a large room on the first floor of the Mansion House, resplendent with red and gold furniture. We chatted together, sitting on an elegant sofa. It was nice to see each other as we had hardly met since our Harrow days, and as the Lord Mayor and the Permanent Secretary gravely exchanged information and views the years fell away and I had an irresistible impression that young Peter Studd was telling young Antony Part about an interesting holiday abroad.

These foreign trips are a great event in a Lord Mayor's term of office and due pomp and decorum are preserved – whenever possible. Sir Hugh Wontner, under whose chairmanship of the Savoy Group I served in my sixties, told me that his trip as Lord Mayor was to Kenya. His party were to stay at a rest house on the Ethiopian border. When Sir Hugh went into the bedroom which he and his wife were to use he found it in process of being wrecked by the local monkeys. 'This did not bother me unduly because we would take a bedroom from one of the Sheriffs.' Calm was restored (except for one of the Sheriffs) and the party went into lunch. Lady Wontner took her seat, reached for the bread roll on her side plate, and was beaten to it by a hairy brown hand. The local monkeys had not heard of the respect due to the Lady Mayoress!

Life at Harrow was not restricted to work and games. The Harrow school songs are widely known. Perhaps the most famous stereotype of Harrow is of several hundred schoolboys in their unique straw hats, flatter than a 'boater' and with a broader brim, flocking up the Hill and converging either on the school yard for 'Bill' (the school roll call), or for some performance in the

Speech Room. To the songs were added in my time some notable schoolboy performances of Gilbert and Sullivan, in which I got no further than the part of prompter.

There were other amateur actors, including Michael Denison, and the future horse show commentator, Dorian Williams. Dorian appeared with considerable distinction as Abraham Lincoln in John Drinkwater's play of that name. In this I stood behind the scenes with a box partly filled with gravel and simulated the sound of marching feet during the singing of 'John Brown's Body'.

To complete a rather unusual threesome, I had an interesting function in the last act of *Cyrano de Bergerac* starring Guy Haslewood, who came from the same house as Michael Denison and Dorian Williams, and in earlier years Terence Rattigan. Future theatrical men seemed to congregate at The Park. In the last act Cyrano visits his great love Roxanne, who has retired to a convent. It is a melancholy autumnal occasion. My job was to sit some thirty feet up in the roof of the Speech Room and drop the leaves that were gently falling. I spent a long time aiming at Cyrano's famous nose but, perhaps fortunately, never scored a direct hit. Later I graduated to more important parts, including playing the lead in a rather deplorable melodrama called *Shameless Wayne*.

Along with amateur acting went a competition in reading aloud and, as a novel undertaking, a competition in reading for radio. All this meant that before leaving Harrow I had been taught something about voice production and public presentation, both of which were of great value much later on for the considerable round of public speaking and appearances that came to be expected of many senior civil servants.

Came the time that I was due to go to Cambridge. At prep school my father had told me that he could not afford to send me to both Harrow and Cambridge and a scholarship to one of them was essential. So I was dismayed when he now said that his financial circumstances had changed for the worse and a scholarship to Cambridge was required. Luckily the age allowance came to my rescue once more and the deed was done in rainy December weather in 1936.

Harrow had not been a happy time for me in spite of considerable success at work and some success at games. Family problems had played their part in my development – or lack of it – and I had not been relaxed enough to learn how to get on with other people as well as I should have done. Moreover, fifty years ago house masters were much more remote characters (and more like a court of last resort) than they are today. However, the essential fault was mine and success in relationships came only in my final year when appointment as a school monitor was reinforced by greater success at games to which Elmfield attached such importance.

My final report from my house master began, 'Although he has not fulfilled his early promise at games, he did become twelfth man to the School Cricket XI. He also won a Scholarship to Trinity College, Cambridge.'

After all this Cambridge came as a great release. The intense concentration on French and German was congenial. The setting at Trinity with its Great Court, the Wren Library and the River Cam running quietly along the Backs was inspiring, and the college was, of course, a much larger society than a house at Harrow, so that one could choose one's friends without embarrassment.

My competitive father was responsible for my taking up the unusual game of real tennis (*jeu de paume*). This he arranged for an entirely ignoble reason: 'Now that you have got a scholarship you must get a Blue at something. I have been finding out the game played by the smallest number of undergraduates. It is real tennis, for which a half-Blue is awarded. So that is what you must take up.' Luckily, real tennis is a fascinating game. Once you have made yourself at home in the complicated court with its lines on the floor, its grille, its tambour, its dedans, its satisfying winning gallery (a shot into the netting of which rings a bell), a ball with no rubber in it and a racket of peculiar shape, this game – of which lawn tennis was a simplification – is physically satisfying and intellectually demanding.

Work, however, was the main theme, and success in it an economic necessity. In this respect my father was never short of initiative, especially when it came to saving money on my education. In my first Easter vacation he arranged for me to be interviewed by his friend the chairman of Shell. Lord Bearsted offered me a job, but said that I would have to leave Cambridge that summer and go out to the Middle East. This offer, completely uncharacteristic of Shell even in those days, failed to persuade me to curtail my happy days at Cambridge.

Back at university I had, just once, a great piece of luck at work. A rather fierce gentleman from Alsace, Baron de Glehn, who taught us composition in our first year, set us one week to translate into French a passage which seemed to be, and was, familiar. Not only had I translated the piece at Harrow but I had a copy of the French version. So I copied this out in short order, sent it in, and went off to play squash. It was returned marked 'gamma ? minus' lower than which one could hardly get. What, I thought, is the value of an expensive public school education if it cannot get me a better mark than that? Then I looked at my Cambridge effort and saw a large question mark alongside the last section. The piece set by Baron de Glehn was eight lines shorter than the piece I had done at Harrow. This experience impelled me, in my career in Whitehall, to be particularly careful about checking the accuracy of documents!

The dons were good in that still small university of some 6000 students. They believed in the then popular maxim that schools were for finding out 'what' whereas universities were for exploring 'whys' and 'wherefores'. They stimulated us in the study of literature, they started us on philosophy and they encouraged us in amateur dramatics. Each year we did a production in German, usually of a major classic, finishing with a version of *Faust* which Goethe wrote when he was in his twenties. It was produced by E. K. (Francis) Bennett, a Senior Tutor at Caius whom we envied his photographs of his glamorous friend Leni Riefenstahl, later to become know as a film director and Hitler's photographer.

Francis had another friend, Emil Preetorius, who ran a famous school of theatrical design in Munich. Preetorius was persuaded to give his students as their project for one term the design of the sets for our production. They had to be simple because we could not afford anything elaborate. They also had to be able to accommodate more than a dozen changes of scene with intervals (except for the main interval) of not more than a minute between each scene. A challenging requirement which was successfully met with the help of an apron stage, half tabs and at the back a choice between a back cloth and a cyclorama.

By coincidence the three leading parts were each performed by people who were later connected with public service. Faust was played by Kit Dodds who went into the Ministry of Defence and later rose to be an Assistant Under-Secretary of State there. Gretchen, the heroine, was portrayed by Elizabeth Langstaff who, as Lady Reed, spent many years in Nigeria with her New Zealand husband Nigel, who ultimately became the Chief Justice of Northern Nigeria. The trio was completed by me as Mephistopheles, a piece of casting affectionately considered as entirely appropriate by my more scurrilous friends. It was a great experience. To spend six months on the text of the German equivalent of *Hamlet* was a fascinating voyage of discovery and of course the actual production, helped by some really good costumes in eighteenth century style, hired from a theatrical costumier in London, was a thrill for us and was kindly received by our audiences.

There was one exception. My father thought it his duty to come. 'I suppose I shall have to go and see Antony act. Which of my family understands any German?' My half sister, Gwen, whose knowledge of the language was not in fact extensive, volunteered. The play begins with a monologue of some ten minutes or more by Faust. Halfway through it my father, whose voice as a member of an audience tended to be audible beyond his neighbour, said to Gwen, 'What is he saying?' He received the classic reply, 'He is going a bit fast for me.' Recollection of his own prowess as an amateur actor, coupled with his marriage to a professional actress, tempered his appreciation of his younger son's performance. True to form (and naturally to my pleasure) my mother, who of course came on a different day to my father, took a different view.

Like many other undergraduates of the day we were not at all martial in our attitudes. We were in favour of disarmament so long as it was mutual and we thought that Hitler's territorial ambitions should be checked, but we believed that this should have been done at an early stage by preventing him from re-occupying the Rhineland.

We had most of us rather disliked the Officers' Training Corps at our schools but we would certainly not have voted for the notorious Oxford University Union motion that 'we will not fight for King and Country'. We had the natural antipathy of youth to some aspects of the existing order but, except for a few, politics were not a consuming interest. And although we listened with admiration to some of Anthony Blunt's lectures on the History of Art we should not have dreamt of adopting his left-wing political attitudes. (He had not, of course, at that stage been unmasked as a spy.)

My time at Cambridge covered the Spanish Civil War and there were certainly some undergraduates who were strongly opposed to Franco, at least one of them going off to fight for the Republicans. On the whole, however, my contemporaries, to the extent that they were not aligned with the establishment, were anti-Conservative rather than positively pro-Socialist. Books which have given the impression that the communist element was large in Cambridge and Trinity do not paint a true picture.

My years at Cambridge contributed further to my acquaintance with foreign countries. This had begun in 1924 when I was eight and my father took my mother, my sister Rosemary and me to Belgium. He showed me the First World War trenches, the awfulness of which made an indelible impression on my young mind and did not help me to welcome the Second World War in 1939. Since that visit to Belgium I have been fortunate to travel abroad in every year but one. Often on holiday, but there was one curious interlude. On my first skiing holiday in Switzerland at the age of nine my father and mother had a blazing row. He returned to London to arms that would welcome him and with indignant enterprise she took Rosemary and me off to Florence as a sort of cultural base with a prospect of schooling.

We left Switzerland in January with the snow thick on the ground. We were in a sleigh with our luggage on a second sleigh attached to the first by a lengthy pole. We began the journey by descending the dramatic Maloja Pass with its dozen or so hairpin bends and were relieved to arrive at the bottom with the second sleigh still attached and all the the luggage intact.

Below the snowline, on flatter ground, we changed into a *carrozza* (an old-fashioned enclosed carriage rather like a miniature stagecoach) with the luggage suitably stacked outside and my mother clutching two outsize boxes of chocolates presented to her by the sympathetic hotel manager. We arrived at the frontier post near Chiavenna, a small hut occupied by two immigration and customs men. They took a close interest in their rare visitors, looked into all the luggage and seemed specially suspicious of the two boxes of chocolates. My mother, who could be a forceful lady when she chose, started – unwisely – to argue with them and in the fracas one of the boxes fell to the floor and the chocolates scattered widely. My mother walked out with the other box leaving the customs men scrabbling for the chocolates from the box on the floor.

As a matter of fact, my mother was not at her best with customs men. Some years later she and I were travelling by rail from Switzerland to Germany. In the fashion of those days she had a large green trunk. After a sharp verbal exchange the German customs officer insisted on making a thorough search of the trunk and unearthed a small brown paper bag. He plunged his hand through the brown paper and drew out a fistful of white substance. 'Ha!' he said with triumph. 'Opium!' It was, in fact, Lux soapflakes!

We stayed in a small *pensione* just up the hill from Florence to Fiesole where the rather grandly entitled 'Chef' had an unusual but satisfying habit. He kept a large supply of empty bottles and when he felt himself getting into a bad temper he would take a few bottles and throw them at a wall at the bottom of the garden. An arrangement, it seems to me, that every office could do with.

Matched only perhaps by the following attractive privilege contained in a jocular certificate presented to me many years later making me an honorary Texan: 'You may wear spurs in the office on Fridays' – useful, perhaps in Whitehall and the City.

The only school available in Florence was unattractive to a nine year old boy: the International Girls' School, which took girls up to eighteen. I did learn a useful amount of Italian there but acquired a life-long hatred of netball and a distaste for girlish attempts to teach me dancing. Both of them appeared to me cissy occupations. But the stay in Florence was put to good cultural use. My mother was a keen believer in Baedeker and she greatly advanced our eduction in art and architecture.

Later, my work for government took me, as it did a good number of my future colleagues, to many different countries – in my case twenty-seven. During my time in the Civil Service my French and German came in useful too, especially in connection with the EEC. It has been fashionable, in the interest of science and technology, to deride the practical usefulness of an arts education to a civil servant's career. Some knowledge of science and technology and some expertise in them are certainly desirable, as I have already suggested, and the general bias towards the arts badly needs correcting. But what in the meantime matters most is the *calibre* of an administrator. It would be no advantage to the Civil Service if they were to exchange top-grade arts graduates for graduates from a pool of scientists, the best of whom have already gone into academic life or research establishments. Perhaps the Royal Society, which is such a magnet to aspiring scientists, should consider amending their requirements so that more people from non-academic occupations should be able to become Fellows.

And then there were girls. One of these was Philippa, the sister of my closest friend Evelyn Talbot-Ponsonby, who later mixed his work for BP with becoming the best translator into English of the twentieth century German poet Stefan George. Phil, like her brother in good looks, not tall but with even features, was not up at Cambridge. But we saw each other in the holidays and she came as my partner to the May Week Ball at Trinity. She also came on the splendid family holiday immediately after my last term at Cambridge. We started in the north of Yugoslavia and moved southwards as far as Dubrovnik before taking a train up to Sarajevo and Belgrade and on to Budapest. We were not well off and the whole eight weeks, travel included, cost £50 a head. At Podgora, a little fishing village, which has grown in recent years into a large tourist resort, the charge was five shillings a day all in and a melon and a bunch of grapes each cost one penny. It was a delight to swim out into the Adriatic in the early evening and turn to watch the setting sun turning the bare hills red.

In the north of the country Phil and I climbed Triglav, the high mountain which stands at the spot where Yugoslavia, Austria and Italy join. At some points the climb was more difficult than we had expected and darkness fell just after we reached the snowline and before the manned hut was in sight. A moment of panic as no trail was visible in the snow and darkness but after a few minutes the lights of the hut appeared and we walked in – to be greeted by a rather rough-looking group of men (possibly smugglers, we thought) sitting down to feed. We were unsure how we would be received but all was well and we were given something to eat. We were shown up to a bedroom with two single bunks. Overcome by a sense of responsibility I did not press matters beyond a chaste goodnight kiss. Who knows, I thought in later years, she might never have been free to make a happy marriage with Sir Peter Scott, the world famous conservationist, if I had been more enterprising on that night on Triglav!

We were awakened at 4 a.m. and set out for the summit, a climb of only moderate difficulty, and reached the top soon after daybreak. Triglav is much higher than any mountain within sight and we saw something which I have never seen since: a thick purple rim round the whole 360° of the horizon. It was wondrous and awe-inspiring.

Just before that memorable holiday I had completed my Cambridge academic career satisfactorily with a first-class honours degree but not without some anxiety about one paper. Halfway through the allotted time for the paper I got stuck and looked up for inspiration at the rafters of the Corn Exchange, which was decorated with Biblical quotations. Unfortunately, the one that met my eye was 'What ye have sown that shall ye reap'!

So in every way Cambridge was a happy time. The growing threat of war and some of our personal circumstances made us less carefree than we might have been, but we had read Robert Louis Stevenson's essay *On Crabbed Age and Youth*:

> Youth is the time to go flashing from one end of the world to the other, both in mind and body; to try the manners of

> different nations; to hear the chimes at midnight; to see the sun rise in town and country; to be converted at a Revival; to circumnavigate the metaphysics and run a mile to see a fire.

Had this been an examination paper most of us would not have scored more than seven marks out of ten, but some of us did sit up for the whole of one night talking about the ways of the world (with an interval for ghost stories between 1 a. m. and 2 a. m.). We did learn to ride a penny-farthing bicycle (very hard to mount) and we did ride a bicycle made for four (difficult for the tail end Charlie, who had to jump on at the start with the bicycle moving and his pedals going round). I also belonged to a light-hearted cricket club which, shortly before my time, claimed to be the only club ever to have taken the whole of the team to an away match in one car.

What to do for work – and money? My father was not going to produce any more cash and my mother was struggling to make both ends meet by taking paying guests to help her pay her debts to the bank, incurred when she bought Ashburn Place from my father at the time of the divorce. I felt I wanted to 'do something' and, therefore, declined the junior academic post for further study that Trinity kindly offered me. The world of business appeared somehow alien to me; 'making a profit' did not seem attractive as a lifetime objective and an interview at ICI did not encourage me. The interviewer told me that, as an arts graduate, my prospects would be limited 'perhaps to something on the personnel side'.

When I was sixteen my parents, on the recommendation of Cyril Norwood, the head master of Harrow, had sent me to the National Institute of Industrial Psychology for some tests. These showed a satisfactorily high IQ and 'a quick mind, organising ability and powers of initiative'. The Institute thought that I might be suitable for the Home Civil Service. 'What,' I remember asking, 'does that do?'

The Civil Service was and is involved in a wide variety of activities from advising Ministers on the development of policies to a very large volume of executive work on the implementation of existing policies. This includes such semi-independent bodies as the Inland Revenue, Customs and Excise and, in the 1930s, the Post Office. Nowadays three-quarters of the non-industrial Civil Service work outside London and nearly half of all civil servants are women.

In the 1930s the Service was severely stratified into the administrative class, who were regarded as the policy-making élite, the executive class (some of them, particularly in the service departments, the Inland Revenue and Customs and Excise, in senior positions), most of whom were engaged in the execution of existing policies, and the clerical class who handled the considerable volume of paper involved. Each had its own entrance examination. This unsatisfactory arrangement lasted until 1968, when the government approved the recommendation of the Fulton Committee that the three classes should be amalgamated. Before this happened it was difficult but not impossible to move up from one class to another; as this narrative will show, four people rose from the lowest rung to the rank of Permanent Secretary.

Then, as now, the administrative class spent most of their time initiating or implementing change. It was – and is – their characteristic function, a point that has been overlooked by a number of prominent people who ought to know better.

In the 1930s the total size of the Service was 150,000. This contrasts with 500,000 today, a figure that illustrates how many controls and incentives successive ministers and parliaments have introduced in the meantime. In the 1930s the administrative class, 2,000 strong, was regarded as a profession and was held in high esteem as a challenging and worthwhile career, particularly at Oxford and Cambridge, which in those days supplied most of the new entrants. This was an unfortunate narrowing of opportunity which has now been largely remedied. All the same, competition to enter the class in the 1930s was quite severe, and for the young graduates of those days it ranked high among the opportunities for employment. Then, as now, some people went into the Service for the guarantee of continuity and the pension at the end (not index-linked until the 1970s). But for many, if not most, it was the challenge and variety of the work that counted. There was also the then highly esteemed opportunity to serve the State in an honourable capacity.

The pay was not munificent. A Permanent Secretary earned £3000 a year and my own starting pay as an Assistant Principal was £275. One reason for remembering that precise figure was that the manager of our local branch of Barclays Bank called off the threat of forcing my mother to sell our home in Ashburn Place on condition that I pledged my salary to the bank as a guarantee of my mother's sustained efforts to reduce her debts. This story had another wry twist. Much later, after her second marriage to my stepfather, she sold the still splendid house for conversion into flats. It fetched the princely sum of £2000 which rather more than covered her debts at the time.

The Home Civil Service seemed the kind of public service that might be congenial and which I might be some good at. So, after some 'cramming', the exam was taken in the summer before the holiday in Yugoslavia, the only disadvantage of the timing being that I missed going to a family dance in the country as the partner, for the first time, of my future wife.

A fourteenth place in the Home Civil Service examination did not guarantee me entry to the department of my choice. Luckily no problem arose. Having failed to appreciate the central role of the Treasury, I did not aspire to that and did the rounds of the Home Office, the Ministry of Health (which also looked after local government in those days) the Ministry of Labour and the Board of Education. Against the advice of Dr Norwood I chose the last as seeming to offer interesting work and the best prospects, and it was regarded as one of the best training grounds in the Service. My application was accepted – and I hope that the acceptance had nothing to do with the fact that the Director of Establishments was the son of the House Master of my father's house, the Knoll, at Harrow, a fact which emerged at my interview at the Board. (It was at the Knoll that my father and Winston Churchill were contemporaries. My father told me that Winston was so unpopular that on one occasion they held him outside a second floor window by his ankles. I am inclined to believe this story, though my father was much prone to exaggeration, particularly about his own exploits, and on this account was known to me in later years as 'the personification of an Unreliable Source'.)

So in October 1937 I presented myself, with some trepidation, at the entrance of a large imposing stone building at the Parliament Square end of Whitehall. I was shown into a large high-ceilinged room with a coal fire and a good view of the Cenotaph. As an Assistant Principal, the lowest grade in the administrative class, I was attached to a tutor, who was among the five people working in the room. As a Principal he was one rank higher than me in the Civil Service.

I was, I suppose, a typical recruit. I was the son of successful middle-class parents and had enjoyed a privileged education at a public school and at Cambridge. My special advantages were a much wider experience of foreign travel than most of my contemporaries had had and a growing interest in management of which I had already had some experience at both Harrow and university. Both of these characteristics, coupled with a developing capability for public speaking, were to play an important part in my career.

It is no use expecting that when you first join the Civil Service you are quickly going to be involved in earth-shaking policy decisions. My first administrative act on my first day was to recommend to my tutor a proposal from a local education authority to buy some land for a modest extension of a school garden.

In 1937 training by a tutor was the only training provided for a new entrant, and with a good tutor such as I had, that counted for a great deal. But as time has gone on things have greatly improved and there are now special induction courses both service-wide and in departments. In the 1930s, however, one had to rely on training on the job. I was put in to help deal with cases from the large (and competent) Local Education Authority for the West Riding of Yorkshire. The authority had to come to us for various approvals including the purchase of land or any proposal to build a new school, or a major extension to one, and so on. It was immediately and forcefully emphasised to me that public money was very scarce and that every proposal must be scrutinised with the utmost rigour. Many of the schools were church schools (Church of England or Roman Catholic) and the respective responsibilities for paying for them and appointing their teachers formed a central focus of argument – often heated argument – between the various parties concerned, until the astute and brilliantly negotiated settlement in the Butler Education Act of 1944.

The Board of Education also provided a useful introduction to the problem of relations between central and local government. In the 1930s it was almost an article of faith that control of education should be exercised primarily by the Local Education Authorities (LEAs) and their teachers.

The idea that control, particularly of the curriculum, should be in the hands of Ministers of the Crown was regarded as abhorrent – and even constitutionally dangerous. The example of Nazi Germany was often cited as an undesirable precedent. Since those days fifty years ago very important changes have occurred in the roles of the Department of Education, the Local Education Authorities and the teachers. As I shall argue later, not all of these have been for the better.

The organisation of local government was a relic of history, but no easier to change on that account. The LEAs ranged from the LCC who – as a matter of policy – did not allow HMIs into their schools, through counties and county boroughs of varying size to some boroughs (Part III Authorities) which controlled only elementary schools. For education to be financed entirely from the rates would, however, have been impracticable, even if some people had thought that desirable, because either the rates would have had to rise to intolerable levels or the education budget would have dominated local authority finance to an undesirable extent – or both. So central government had to play *some* part. The majority view at this time was that it should be minimised and it was a piece of deliberate terminology that the relevant department of central government should be called a *Board* rather than a *Ministry* of Education. The administrators, therefore, had few responsibilities for the education that went on in the schools. Any such advice from the centre – and it was only advice – was the province of HM Inspectors, constitutionally independent of the Board and based in each locality. The HMIs also advised the Board's administrators and acted as their eyes and ears in the schools.

I had never seen an elementary or secondary school – or, indeed any publicly provided place of education – and one could not get a very graphic picture from the files or from reading the advice of the HMIs. I asked if I could go and see some schools in the West Riding and was, to my astonishment, refused. 'No,' they said, 'because if you were to visit some schools you might begin to think you knew something about it and that would be very dangerous! The HMIs are your advisers on the ground.' This was not so daft as it sounded because if one visited, say, half a dozen schools one's vision of elementary and secondary schools would be based on that small sample alone.

However, I was allowed to go, with an HMI as a guide, and ever since then I have been the strongest believer in getting civil servants out of their offices to see what the places that they are concerned with are really like – to get to know the people involved, what their views are and what makes them tick. The Civil Service should not be, and is not today, a cloistered community remote from the real world. This is especially desirable for the Treasury whose work does not give its staff a very wide range of contacts. This point of view is now widely accepted in the Service, though the degree of knowledge and understanding varies. At any rate one would be surprised to find anyone today who still believes in the dictum of the War Office financiers of the late 1930s: 'Never visit an establishment or you will want to give it money.'

But visits on any large scale are not feasible for everybody, even in the administrative class, and visits are not enough to give the Service a full understanding of the ways of the prime movers, whether in the public or the private sector. Exchanges are difficult to arrange because the needs and opportunities of the two parties seldom coincide neatly enough. But secondments are better and some of us have been energetic in promoting them for the last twenty years or so. In 1985 some 230 civil servants were seconded into commercial and industrial organisations and 450 into other organisations such as local and health authorities, universities overseas, government and EEC institutions, making a total of 680. In the opposite direction secondments into the Service numbered some 155 from the private sector and 255 from the public sector, totalling 380. My successor at the Department of Trade and Industry, Sir Peter Carey, added a useful dimension when he was able to arrange for a few of his staff to become non-executive directors of wholly-owned subsidiaries of companies with which they had no official dealings.

My own first visit, in 1937, was to Keighley in the West Riding. My companion and guide was an HMI, Leonard Gibbon. I could not then know that he and I would be closely and constructively associated after the war in the massive expansion and development of school building. The school in Keighley was a Roman Catholic school and everyone was carefully drilled for the occasion. In the first classroom that we entered forty young voices, speaking in unison, greeted us with 'Good morning, Sirs.' On this visit there was too much formality for me to learn very much, except to see what kind of people the teachers seemed to be, to get an impression of classes of forty children (all sitting in serried ranks in those days) and to see the physical state of the buildings. A most notable place in that particular building was the underground playground, the floor being considerably broken up by quite numerous iron pillars supporting the structure of the building. The pillars gave rise to a remarkable mixture of ingenuity and confusion when the children played football!

The Divisional Inspector, a rank senior to Leonard Gibbon, accompanied us on some of the drives around the beautiful hilly countryside. He brought his small daughter with him. She produced an attractively original metaphor which has stuck in my mind ever since. As the car moved up a long straight road she asked, 'Daddy, is this one of those hills that lies down as you go up it?'

It always paid to keep one's eyes and ears open. At the very least one learned something about human nature and tactical devices. My tutor, John Burrows, took me up to Yorkshire when he was asked to adjudicate between two grammar schools on a subject I don't now recall; I rather think it was connected with rival claims for an extension to take in more pupils. Burrows and I sat in the local Town Hall in rather ornate wooden pews with our backs to the wall. In front of us, at each of two tables, sat the representatives of the contestants, the chairman and the clerk to the Governors of each school. Each table was covered with a blue cloth which did not, however, extend very far over the edge of the table on our side.

The chairman of one set of governors made a reasonably good case and raised some questions which the other side clearly needed to answer. The second chairman rose to his feet. Not only was he ineffective, he was inaccurate; and we could see his clerk kicking him on the shins each time a misguided point was made.

Tactics and human nature became an inexhaustible mine of interest for me. The contacts between the Board of Education (and its successor departments) and the Local Education Authorities were a fruitful source. My generation inherited the (true) story of a deputation in the early thirties from a Part III authority that was responsible only for elementary schools, about the purchase of some land for a new school. The authority's area was quite close to Manchester. The land they wanted to buy was so waterlogged that the water was actually shown on the map of the locality. The very courteous civil servant receiving the deputation drew attention to this fact. The Chairman of the Authority replied, 'Oh, Mr Eaton, dost tha mean that pond? Let me tell thee that in actual fact that pond is so small that one of t'elephants at t'zoo in Bellevue could sup it up in twice!' Persuasive though this was, the purchase was not approved.

The day to day working at the Board might have seemed rather dull and legalistic if it had not been new to me. It was concerned mainly with the administration of the law, particularly the Education Act 1921, in rather a formal fashion in times of parsimony. But it gave me a good grounding under very demanding supervison. Senior to my tutor, John Burrows, was Gilbert Flemming, a shy, but intelligent man who, after an agonisingly long time because of the age structure of the department after the First World War, became a distinguished Permanent Secretary of the Ministry in the 1950s. His standards were high. He very seldom uttered a word of praise, but when he did you knew that you had deserved it. He was rigorously accurate. Commenting on one of my draft letters he said, 'The Board don't "feel" – they "think"!'

My other experience during what turned out to be a short period of some eighteen months at the Board of Education was to be made secretary of an internal committee on adult education. This is the type of experience that the top management of government departments like to give to promising young men. It enables them to meet more senior officials (and often outsiders), to get to know a different side of the department's work and to cut their teeth on committee work, which inevitably plays a big part in a large organisation such as a government department with its many dealings with other departments and with other bodies not only in Britain but overseas. The Adult Education Committee lasted only a few months for me. I don't think I did particularly well, being too prone to think that the whole problem could be solved by a few hours' hard thinking, preferably by the secretary to the committee! Luckily this piece of youthful arrogance was put down to inexperience.

So up to this time my apprenticeship had been served in a settled environment, political, legislative and financial. It was clear that in order to survive adequately as a civil servant one needed an intelligence high enough to master such matters as the complexities of the Education Acts and an aptitude for applying oneself to accurate detail.

In those days civil servants did not get out of their offices much and in that sense they were a monastic order, but not one out of touch with the world of public education. Through HMIs and deputations from authorities, teachers and churches they were well informed, as they demonstrated during the war when, under the Permanent Secretary, Sir Maurice Holmes, they drafted the Green Book which led directly to the Butler Act of 1944.

Like everyone else at that time, except a few people like R. S. (later Sir Robert) Wood, they underestimated the importance of technical education, which was regarded as a rather esoteric low-level subject related largely to craft apprenticeship. There were, however, some notable exceptions among the colleges themselves such as the Polytechnic, Regent Street, and the Birmingham College of Technology. This was, so to speak, the private enterprise sector of education because its supply was closely related to voluntary demand, and in the late 1930s the demand was not very great.

Even in a book about the Civil Service it may seem odd to leave the ministers until last, but the fact is that at that stage in the history of public education the political element at national level was not important. Indeed, in a certain constitutional sense it was important that it should be unimportant. So the Board of Education tended to be used as a convenient parking place for people like peers, who were of value to the government for other reasons.

Before my time the Earl of Halifax, the future Foreign Secretary, was President. His Private Secretary was Griffith (G.G.) Williams, later to rise to Deputy Secretary. Able, and a lively conversationalist with a good sense of humour, he was honoured by an invitation to Garrowby, Lord Halifax's home in Yorkshire, for a weekend. The prospect of this grandeur rather intimidated him. He did not have the courage to ask in advance whether he should wear tails or a dinner jacket for dinner, so he took both. When the time came to change he still lacked this important information. He decided to wait until at least some of the company were likely to be assembled and then to creep down the stairs in his dressing gown and look through the keyhole of the drawing room. He achieved this and was just about to stand up after acquiring the necessary evidence when a voice behind him said, 'May I help you, Sir?' It was the butler. Such are the inhibitions inspired by protocol and class distinction.

Class distinction of a different sort was a marked feature of the Civil Service of the day. These distinctions have, over time, become more blurred at the edges, but as in the Army some hierarchical distinctions are inevitable. It was possible – but difficult – to move up from one class to another. Nevertheless a few people have gone all the way from the lowest grade to become a full Permanent Secretary and sole Head of Department.

The first was Sir Douglas Lovelock, who rose from Clerical Officer in the Treasury via the DTI (in my time there) to become Chairman of the Board of Customs and Excise. On his retirement from the Civil Service he became First Church Estates Commissioner. The second was Sir Terence Heiser, who rose from Clerical Officer in the Colonial Office to be Permanent Secretary of the Department of the Environment.

In a slightly different setting Sir John Lang, by some years their senior, worked his way up from the lowest grade in the Service to become Secretary to the Admiralty alongside the First Sea Lord. Most recently Sir Gordon Manzie has risen from the grade of Clerical Officer to become, as a Second Permanent Secretary, Chief Executive of the Property Services Agency. He also served in the DTI.

Early in 1939 an important change in my life occurred. In preparation for the all too likely war the Ministry of Supply was to be formed. Its task was to supply the armed forces with most of their needs except food and drink. I was sent there to be Assistant Private Secretary to the First Minister of Supply Elect, Leslie Burgin, a solicitor, who – as a National Liberal – had just come into the new coalition government. The formation of the Ministry of Supply was a huge task. It was meticulously planned well in advance. It involved putting together large parts of each of the three service departments, the Royal Ordnance factories and similar establishments, civil servants from other departments (including the Board of Trade) and the largest influx into government of senior businessmen that has ever been seen.

The function of the businessmen was to head various parts of the department, with the work of which they were widely experienced, particularly raw materials controls. This impressive invasion included such eminences as Lord Woolton in charge of equipment and stores, Sir Andrew Duncan of steel, Oliver Lyttleton of non-ferrous metals and Sir Cecil Weir of explosives. Other notable figures were Lord Layton from the *News Chronicle* and Patrick (later Sir Patrick) Ashley-Cooper from the Bank of England.

There were also senior officers from the armed services – Rear Admirals, Major-Generals and Air Vice-Marshals – who headed other divisions. Among notable younger men was Oliver Franks, a don from Oxford, who, with his luminous intelligence, was to become one of the most distinguished figures in British public life.

The headquarters was in the Adelphi Building, an ungainly but modern structure which still stands south of the Strand and facing over the Thames. When I joined the future department it had a staff of twelve, including the Minister and the telephone operator and the legislation to create it had not yet passed through Parliament. When I left in June 1940, 100,000 people were working for it. Many people outside the Ministry (and some people inside it) had little idea what its range of responsibilities was. From one firm we received in the Private Office a letter addressed to the Minister saying, 'We should like to be considered as suppliers to the Armed Forces of the items listed below. As an indication of the quality of our products we enclose samples of our ring doughnuts.' The Minister never did get to see the samples, nor were they forwarded, as strictly they should have been, to the Ministry of Food. They made a welcome addition to our coffee breaks in the Private Office.

The general atmosphere at this time was uncomfortable. Mr Chamberlain's flight to Munich to see Hitler had taken place six months earlier and he still hoped for peace. It was not possible to get out of 10 Downing Street any decisive support for preparations for war. For a youthful Private Secretary experiences in widely differing subjects were being accumulated almost too fast. It was also fascinating to see the Foreign Office telegrams, particularly those to and from Berlin. Working directly for a Minister, and a busy Minister at that, was a marvellous professional education, and this was aided by the imperturbable wisdom of the Permanent Secretary, Sir Arthur Robinson and by my experienced and genial Principal Private Secretary, H. H. Sellar.

Top visitors could be very sensitive. A visit to the Minster from Sir Walter Citrine, the General Secretary of the TUC, was correctly thought to be important. He turned round at the entrance to the Adelphi and left before his interview when he was asked to fill in a security pass. I should have filled in the form and gone down to meet him and asked him just to sign it. One lesson learned without any very serious reprimand.

As a Private Secretary you never know who is going to ring you up. One day I had just put the telephone down after arranging for a Peer to come to see the Minister with his ideas about a new battle tank when the telephone immediately rang again. (There is nearly always one telephone conversation going on in a private office. In my days as Permanent Secretary of the Department of Trade and Industry in the 1970s one person was engaged almost full time on arranging meetings in Whitehall or outside appointments.)

The cockney voice of my caller (the frequent swear words are omitted) said, 'Is that the Private Secretary to the Minister of Supply? I thought there was supposed to be a shortage of . . . paper in this country!' 'Yes, there is,' I said, 'and there is a control over its manufacture and use.' 'Well why don't the . . . controllers get off their . . . arses and do some controlling?' 'Could you tell me what the particular problem is?' 'Do you know where I have just been?' 'No. If you could tell me it might help.' 'I have just been to the . . . dogs,' and, in explanation, 'at the . . . White City.' 'Yes, and what happened to annoy you?' 'I was so . . . angry. Do you know what they had there? . . . paper programmes! Why don't you do something about it?' Although I was not clear how paper programmes could be avoided I said, 'I will look into it at once.' I rang off and I am afraid that I failed to take his name and address. Luckily he must have been content to be able to let off steam to someone supposedly in authority.

The legislation to create the Ministry of Supply was duly passed. The efforts which had gone into planning it and bringing it into existence were very considerable, but the pace of rearmament was not. This was due partly to the continued lack of any sense of urgency from the Prime Minister, even after the German invasion of Czechoslovakia and partly to the fact that Leslie Burgin, though capable and a very nice man to work for, had not the exceptional strength of personality to impose himself on the whole operation as Lord Beaverbrook was later able to do. In a way this comparison is unfair because Burgin was working before war had broken out and during the days of the 'phoney war' there was no fighting, whereas Beaverbrook started to operate in the supreme crisis of the Battle of Britain.

With dignified reluctance Mr Chamberlain declared war on Germany at 11.00 a. m. on Sunday 3rd September 1939. I heard the announcement over the radio at the Ministry of Supply in the presence of the Minister. Mr Chamberlain's remarks were followed immediately by the sound of the air-raid sirens. 'Typical of the Germans,' said Mr Burgin as he led us down to the air-raid shelter. As is well known, the air-raid warning turned out to be a false alarm.

After the declaration of war Mr Attlee brought the Labour Party into a national government and Mr Herbert Morrison replaced Mr Burgin as Minister of Supply. He was, of course, a very senior member of the party, well-known for his work at the LCC and his ideas about the way to nationalise industries. He was also reported to be the originator of the advice to a new Minister to 'say "No" to something, however small, on your first day in order to mark your authority.' I don't remember what he picked on at the Ministry of Supply, probably something to do with the way that cases should be presented to him.

Supplying the armed forces was not really his scene (he once asked me what a Bofors gun was) and as only the Assistant Private Secretary I was not able to learn from him anything like as much about the Labour Party as Miss Ellen Wilkinson taught me in 1945. After less than a year as the Minister of Supply he was moved across to be Home Secretary, a post much better suited to his considerable talents.

The Ministry of Supply provided a more complex and large-scale experience than did the Board of Education of people of different professional origins working together – or failing to do so. Also of inter-departmental jealousies. The Personal Assistant to the Director-General of Munitions Production brought with him from the War Office a file of papers that he thought might represent useful ammunition against the people in his old department who were now responsible for writing Operational Requirements for the Army – to be passed to the Ministry of Supply for turning into hardware. These 'amiable feuds', as I later came to call them, are common in large outfits (and in many small ones too, come to that). The task of top management is to see that they are over-ridden by a wider loyalty to objectives that are clearly stated and broadly accepted throughout the organisation. It is this capability in both civilian and military life which distinguishes great leaders or managers from mediocre ones.

Nineteen forty was to prove full of incident for me. The first event was my engagement on January 29, to be followed on a rainy March 26 by marriage. It was one of the last white weddings in wartime London. My bride, Ella, was short, fair and with features that could look solemn, but with a sense of humour that has blossomed through the years and has made her never afraid to speak her mind. She had become a ballet dancer and trained with her much-loved Phyllis Bedells and under some notable Russian teachers. She then joined the Markova-Dolin Ballet of the 1930s and was honoured to dance in two ballets produced for them by Madame Nijinska, sister of the great Nijinsky.

The ballet is an occupation that tends to attract girls with good figures and beautiful legs – and Ella was no exception. In life off-stage you can often spot that someone has had a training in ballet by the way that she moves and by the grace of her arm gestures. As Ella has done, many of them retain these attractions throughout their lives.

She became interested in dancing at the age of ten when she was still at her convent school in Berkshire. It was clear that she was good at it and she made friends with Felicity (Felix) Andreae, who later became a stimulating teacher of ballet and wrote a well-known book and television programme called *Ballet For Beginners*. Ella's father disapproved of his daughter's dancing ambitions and her mother, of whom she was very fond, having died there was no-one to gainsay his attitude.

Fortunately, however, she was befriended by Felix and by Felix's father and mother and was, in effect, adopted by them, so close did the bond become. It was Alex Andreae who escorted her up the aisle at Chelsea Old Church at the end of March. Alex was an outstandingly good-looking man, by then white-haired, who had to give up his career as a Unitarian Minister on the outskirts of Manchester because he became very deaf in his early forties. Luckily there was money in the family (his mother was a Kleinwort) and he was able to bring up his four daughters and befriend Ella at the same time.

I first met Ella through Felix, whom I saw doing a solo cabaret turn (a Blues, I remember) at a party organised by the British Consulate in Paris for vacation students at the Sorbonne from

British universities. I was impressed by Felix's dark good looks and grace of movement, but she had other – and better – romantic attachments and, though we remained affectionate friends for fifty years, the chief benefit that I got from knowing her was meeting Ella and the wise and admirable Alex.

Alex was a staunch ally when the time of my engagement drew near. My mother was a firm supporter of this development and so was my sister Rosemary. But my father, who had grander ideas for me of an unspecific kind, objected that, at twenty-three, I was too young to marry, in which – as a text book might say – there was some truth. However, Ella and I very much wanted to get married (as did many other young couples in wartime) and I persuaded my father to go and talk to Alex.

My father stated his objection and counselled delay. Then Alex: 'One must respect your point of view, Mr Part. I am curious to know at what age you yourself got married.' My father: 'Let me see now, I was twenty-three.' He had chosen the wrong ground to fight on. In the end he gave in with a good grace and, after a considerable row at an early stage, when she (rightly) accused him of being a bully, he became very fond of Ella. Indeed, he employed her for a time at our family shop, General Trading Company, then just off Park Lane, while I was in the Middle East during the war. He liked to go up to her small office with his exiguous sandwich lunch, put his feet up on the sofa and say 'Now whose character shall we pull to pieces today?'

His nice, conscientious secretary had married and was due to have a baby. After rather over eight months of pregnancy she told him that she really would have to leave the GTC to have the baby. Staff for such a shop was hard to come by at that time so he proposed a different, though impractical, course of action. 'You can't do that. You go over to St George's Hospital and have it in your own time.' In later life his affection was chiefly reserved for his Cairn terrier. From his flat in Kensington he and Jock would proceed across Hyde Park to Park Lane. If my father had a date at short notice in the evening he would summon a taxi, put Jock in it on his own, and when the apparently empty taxi arrived at the block of flats where my father lived the porter would open the door, let Jock out and summon the housekeeper to pay the fare.

Back in March 1940 Ella and I went down to Eastbourne for our honeymoon. I had ignorantly supposed that hotels had their own approved arrangements for supplying food to their guests. Not so. There still exists a letter that I wrote to my mother which followed a lyrical description of the happiness that Ella and I were enjoying with the request: 'There is one thing missing – could you please send me my meat ration book without delay?' Our marriage took place under the shadow of my being called up into one of the services. In the end fate and the War Office granted us three months. A particular problem seemed to confront me. I had no special qualifications for the Royal Navy or the RAF, so it looked like the Army. Again, I was not particularly qualified to be a Sapper, a Gunner or a Cavalryman and, of course, there was no question of my going into the Army as an officer. There was nothing to do but wait, and I believe to this day that someone at the War Office, possibly after a good lunch, looked down the list of men to be called up and deliberately spared me from becoming Private Part, which would have been too much for any NCO to resist. I was posted in the middle of June to the Royal Ulster Rifles. The great value of this experience was that it gave me a worm's eye view of life and strongly affected my ideas about management for ever after.

CHAPTER TWO

The Impact of War

'We're too . . . late!' We were walking across the forecourt of Euston Station on 18 June 1940. My companion was a fellow recruit to the ranks of the Royal Ulster Rifles and we had just spotted the newspaper placards announcing the evacuation from Dunkirk. Fortunately he turned out to be wrong, but on that day he was not alone in his forecast.

We were a party of some 200 Londoners of all sorts and sizes bound for the unlikely destination of Ballymena. After sailing from Stranraer to Larne, we arrived at Ballymena station the following morning and were greeted by the Silver Band of the regiment, who marched smartly in front of a rather apprehensive bunch of recruits in civilian clothes, each with a small suitcase, and led us up the hill to begin our transformation into soldiers.

There was not, in the modern jargon, an immediate 'meeting of minds' between the regular soldiers and the civilians. Being shouted at by NCOs was a new experience for the majority. 'Never been spoken to like that in my . . . life before,' said one of my companions. The army was sometimes puzzled in its turn. An officer went round our hut asking each man individually what he did in Civvy Street. He was all right with the first man, who was a lorry driver, and the second, who was a carpenter, but he was visibly startled by the third man who replied, 'I am a guillotine cutter, Sir.' The officer's mind had apparently gone to the French Revolution rather than the paper trade. It was my turn to be startled when the officer reacted to my description of my job with, 'Oh well, I expect we can find you a job in the company office.'

In a short time the Royal Ulster Rifles turned us into quite passable imitations of soldiers. We certainly became very fit probably, in my case, fitter than at any time since – and shoes for PT were, of course, forbidden for 'you soft lot of townees.' We were drilled on the parade ground at the quick pace of the Rifle Regiments originally designed for men much shorter than most of us were. We learned fieldcraft in that gently rolling country of small farms interspersed with woodlands, but in three months we were only allowed to shoot on one occasion owing to shortage of ammunition.

We were a mixed bunch, mainly young men from London already well acquainted with the sole conversational adjective. In the same squad were several potential officers who had volunteered from Dublin and among the others Stanley Adams, who was a member of the Magic Circle and who, along with Peter Follis, a rising young actor, became a star in the revue that C Company staged. Stanley also explained to me how to do the trick of tearing up a large piece of paper, apparently at random, and finishing with the complicated badge of the Ulster Rifles, which included a harp and a bare-breasted woman.

The squad included a nice man called Frank Benemy, whose colour was a genetic throwback in his family for four generations. In later weeks he was included in the group who were chosen by the officers at Ballymena as candidates for training for a commission. The final interview took place at district HQ in Belfast. When Frank's turn came he was marched in front of the panel of interviewing officers – and then, on account of his colour – marched straight out again. We were outraged but could do nothing about it. He did eventually get his commission but the Army made him wait for years rather than months.

This incident of flagrant racial discrimination, which was not outlawed until many years later, made a deep impression on me.

The corporal in charge of our hut was a regular called Hyndman. He had an engaging habit of demonstrating how he was going to report to an officer after he had won the

High Decoration that he regarded as inevitable. March up, stamp the feet to a halt, salute smartly and say firmly and loudly, 'Corporal Hyndman, VC, Sah!' The sergeant was more modest. He contented himself with the announcement to us that he was 'the Welterweight Champion of India and everywhere east of it!'.

After a fortnight or three weeks I was made up to lance-corporal and quickly learned an invaluable lesson. It had been a tiring day and when the time came for bed I was among the first to go to sleep. I was wakened with much clatter by a senior NCO. One of the squad had failed to fix securely the blackout curtain by his bed and a small chink of light was visible to the outside world. Corporal Hyndman was on leave and I was in charge of the hut. The NCO pointed out to me in no uncertain terms that I should have checked the blackout before going to sleep. I was put on a charge the following morning and was paraded in front of the officer who had gone round the hut speaking to each of us soon after we arrived. I pleaded guilty and was admonished. From all this I learned that before a man in charge of others looks after his own needs he must check that all is in order and that the needs of his men have been met. Although this is not precisely mirrored in civilian life, in principle the duty remains analogous.

The officer then asked, 'What did you tell me the other day that your job in Civvy Street was?' 'Assistant Private Secretary to the Minister of Supply, Sir.' His answer took me aback especially as my respect for rank had just been reinforced by my disagreeable experience. 'Good God,' he said, 'really? I thought you were pulling my leg.' Shortly afterwards a potential officers' squad was formed and several from my hut were drafted into it. In the established army fashion we were given a much harder time than we had before but the effect was good.

All the time the importance of our rifle was emphasised. 'You must learn to love your rifle better than your wife.'

The pride of the Ulster Rifles was very great. Later, in North Africa, one of their Battalions was informed that for the final attack on Tunis it was to make up an improvised Brigade with two Battalions of the Guards. Their reaction on hearing the news was characteristic. 'This will be a very fine experience for the Guards.'

In September, before leaving for the OCTU at Dunbar with some of my friends, I was given a few days leave to be with my wife. My father pulled my leg about the contrast between her life in wartime London and the 'idyllic peace' of Ballymena. In this he was more justified than in October 1943 when he wrote to me just before the Battle of Alamein (though he didn't know it), 'I hope you are enjoying the wide open spaces of the Desert while your wife and I are bearing the brunt of the war in London.'

The worm's eye view of life at Ballymena had a lasting effect on me. As a public schoolboy I had had no contact with my fellowmen who had been brought up in less fortunate circumstances and if only because less than five per cent of the population go to private schools this was a bad thing. After the war National Service provided this link, but apart from other considerations expense would not allow it to continue. I do not suppose that non-military National Service could ever be made compulsory, but is there not a strong case for promoting the mix in as many kinds of voluntary service as can be managed?

The other lesson was to be impressed by the lack of understanding that management often has – or seems to have – of those who are managed. Too many people in responsible positions are too slow to learn that you cannot command loyalty: you can only deserve it. Since the war the armed forces have done much better than anyone else in creating a team spirit and a common sense of commitment at all levels. This can be done only if the creative energies of both managers and managed are released in pursuit of objectives that are generally accepted.

The Army in particular are very skilful in forming 'human building blocks' as it were: platoons, companies, battalions, brigades and so on up. This enables them to create a focus of loyalty at each level which is understood by the men who are members of each team.

In the Civil Service individual departments have for long had distinctive characteristics, but it is only in the last twenty years or so that management has begun to be taken more seriously. It may have been more than a coincidence that this started to happen when those who had wartime experience in the Services were reaching the top ranks of the Civil Service. This, however, was only a start. The Fulton Report of 1968 reinforced the trend, but it was not until Mrs Thatcher, with the help of Derek (now Lord) Rayner, caused a special emphasis to be placed on efficiency that management became more widely accepted in the Civil Service as having a high priority.

Back in October 1940 our party of officer cadets found themselves at Dunbar, mostly in hostile weather that blew in from the Firth of Forth. On guard duty at night we needed five thicknesses of clothing and on one occasion our squad marched down the little High Street in the face of a wind so strong that we could lean against it. Much of the parade ground was covered in a thick coating of ice and the sergeant-major, who had come from being a drill sergeant in the Guards, yelled at us from 50 yards away – 'The trouble with you lot is that you are afraid of falling over.' All too true: but his advice, 'Put your feet down firm and flat,' came in useful in later life as well as on the parade ground. He did us proud and we had much pleasure in inviting him out to dinner before we left.

During this time I was recruited into the Intelligence Corps, no doubt on account of my knowledge of German, and on leaving Dunbar was sent for a short time to the Corps depot at Oxford and then on, via the School of Military Intelligence at Matlock, to a specialist course at Cambridge. This involved a study of the set-up in the German army, of German military documents and something of an introduction to the skills of interrogation in the field.

These skills did not accord with the image conveyed by films and television of a fierce interrogator, preferably dressed in something approaching a German SS uniform and threatening the prisoner with unmentionable horrors if he did not cooperate. All soldiers when taken prisoner, in whatever circumstances, feel ashamed. They feel that they have 'let the side down'. They hear a foreign language spoken by all around them. They are not necessarily very gently treated and they cannot be entirely certain that the protective provisions of the Geneva Convention will hold good for them in practice.

In a year in the Western Desert, partly spent in interrogating German prisoners in the field, I never once found an officer who would give away any information, except – as he was required to do – his name, rank and number. But fortunately NCOs were different. On reaching the interrogator they were spoken to for the first time since their capture in their own language and felt a kind of psychological release – and usually an inclination to talk. The inducement was all the greater because their interrogator could demonstrate that he knew more about the battle than they did and this enabled him to lead them on to give more information.

Nevertheless, the first requirement for an interrogator is to impose his personality on the prisoner and that proved to be quite a difficult art for a twenty-five year old to learn, even though the language presented no problem. Usually encouragement was the only way to get people talking, but occasionally a surprise tactic worked. Not long before the Battle of Alamein we at 30 Corps were keen to know whether 164 Infantry Division had arrived from Crete. Our people captured an NCO whom they thought might be from that division. He was brought to me and we sat facing each other on empty petrol cans outside my Armoured Command Vehicle.

'What's your name?' Answer given
'What's your rank?' Answer given
'What's your number?' Answer given
'What's your Division?'
'Do I have to answer that?'
'Of course.' It was an order from an officer.
'164 Division.'

It would be nice to claim that this represented an important intelligence breakthrough but I think that Montgomery probably already had the information from Ultra.

After completing the course at Cambridge I was immediately sent back there as an instructor under the kindly eye of Major Gerald Wellesley, the future Duke of Wellington. Also on the staff were the brother of Alvar Liddell, the well-known BBC news reader, and Goronwy Rees. Goronwy, who was a clubbable man, was not then surrounded by the tentacles of suspicion of being a spy which subsequently assailed him.

At this point, unknown to me, influence was exerted. My uncle, Dealtry Part, shortly to become Lord Lieutenant of Bedfordshire, spoke to his friend Willoughby Norrie, the then Major-General in command of First Armoured Division, and persuaded him to take me on to his intelligence staff. This was arranged and in a letter thanking him, which General Norrie later showed me, my uncle wrote: 'Kick his bottom when necessary.' General Norrie didn't do that, but he later wrote to my uncle 'He must learn to suffer fools more gladly.' He told me that too. This was my first experience of a cohesive military team. The personality of their commander represented a focus of loyalty. 'The Squire', as he was known, was to prove to be not the greatest General in the world but he was the kind of man for whom people would go anywhere and do anything. This ability to inspire loyalty is just as valuable in the Civil Service and business as it is in the Armed Services.

After a short time we moved from Brockham Park in Surrey to the Chippenham area and Ella was allowed to go to nearby Bath to work in the Admiralty in a role which my father described with his usual derisive amiability as 'the lowest form of animal life'.

In August 1941 the First Armoured Division was posted to the Middle East. It was a low point in the fortunes of Britain. When I was due to move to Liverpool to embark on a big liner for the voyage round the Cape, Ella and I, like many other couples, were not sure that we would ever see each other again. We embraced in farewell at her digs and walked down as far as Pulteney Bridge together on her way to her office in Pulteney Street. We had resolved that we would part on the bridge and never look back. The pain of parting was very great. Perhaps it was as well that there was no alternative.

Once aboard some of us leant on the rail and watched others walk up the gangway. To our surprise they included a small party from the Women's Services. One of my brother officers remarked, 'I don't think much of that lot'. 'Never mind' said his more experienced neighbour, 'they'll all be beautiful in a fortnight.' And indeed they were, though opportunities for fraternisation were more strictly controlled than some of the more enterprising officers cared for.

Between July 1941, when our convoys arrived in Durban, and the autumn of 1944 when the Civil Service reclaimed me, experiences and impressions crowded in thick and fast, as they did for many civil servants of my generation. A week visiting the Kruger Park, with elephants, lions, impala and Kudu buck roaming free. Back in Durban two more carefree weeks of feminine company, squash and going to the races. At the end a message from General Norrie that on the sad death in an air crash of the commander of 30 Corps in the desert he, as the new commander, wanted me to join his intelligence staff. Then a flight by flying boat from Durban to Cairo in four stages, landing dramatically on the River Nile at teatime.

Straight into the desert, serving with soldiers like the super-efficient but friendly future Field Marshal Lord Carver who had forgotten more about matters mechanical than I would ever learn. The desert not at all like the sands of Hollywood films (fortunately, for they would have been impassable), but a surface of varying roughness and, except for a few dramatic escarpments, mostly near the coast, small rises and falls in the ground. The preferred tactic was for a tank to be positioned hull down behind one of these rises with only its turret exposed to any approaching enemy. Twenty five years later, as Permanent Secretary to the Ministry of Public Building and Works, I visited Tobruk on business and took the opportunity to look at the Commonwealth War Graves Cemetery, impeccably kept as such cemeteries are. Then a short drive out into the desert for old time's sake, to be faced with one of those sinister rises in the ground. The sense of immediacy was startling. Memories – some sad, some happy – came flooding back.

Shortly after my arrival in the desert my immediate superior sent me and my driver out for experience of the conditions. We were to drive across country for ten miles to a particular spot on the map where we would find the HQ of another formation. We set the compass, with due allowance for the deviations in which we had been instructed, and drove for ten miles on that compass bearing. On arrival, nothing in sight. I don't know what mistake we made, but the memory of the experience returned to me when I heard later of the military maxim 'The Commander who knows where he is usually wins the battle.' This is not the place to re-tell the well-known story of the swirling desert campaign of Rommel versus The Rest and – ultimately – Monty. But a characteristic picture remains of formations of tanks, widely spaced against possible air attack, moving across the desert like a fleet at sea and, like that fleet, liable to be attacked from any point of the compass.

A few more snapshots. Back at Alamein after the spectacular swings of fortune (mostly against us) we re-grouped and trained under General Montgomery. The great attack was to begin at 21.40 hours with a prolonged artillery barrage. At 21.39 hours there was complete silence over the desert. One minute later the sound of a thousand British guns, which could be heard in Alexandria fifty miles away. One minute later still the eerie sound of the bagpipes playing the Highland Division into their night attack.

And then at the end of that long, exhausting battle the final attempt to break the enemy line conclusively. On that night I tuned in to the radio network of the South African Armoured Car Regiment which had the task, if there were a breakthrough, of driving fast to the enemy airfields to try to do important damage there. They were to come up once an hour on the hour if they had any news to report. At midnight nothing. At 1 a.m. – at 2 a.m. – at 3 a.m. nothing. At 4 a.m. a single sentence spoken in a strong South African accent, 'Clear country ahead!' In that memorable moment we knew that the Battle of Alamein was won, that most of the Italians could not retreat for lack of transport, and that at long last the Germans would have to go back hundreds, if not thousands, of miles. Tripoli was not in sight, still less Tunis, but a crucial victory had been won.

Soon afterwards for me, departure from the desert, appointment as the rather over-grandly named Commandant of the Middle East Intelligence Training School near Cairo, followed by promotion to lieutenant colonel to head the intelligence staff of the Corps HQ planning the invasion of the Dodecanese. Then suddenly when the force for that invasion was drastically cut to a size which guaranteed failure, return to England flying in a single hop from Cairo to Gibraltar and then on to England. After a night flight over dark and seemingly hostile seas I looked out in the early morning and glimpsed through the clouds and the rain the English countryside. They were the first green fields I had seen for two years and at the age of twenty six emotion at the sight was, perhaps, permissible.

Then the happiness of reunion with my wife in London. She was lucky to have survived the blitz in Bath. She had been staying in the Francis Hotel. She went down from her bedroom high up at one end of the hotel to the so-called air-raid shelter on the ground floor at the other. A bomb destroyed the half of the hotel in which she had been sleeping and all her belongings too.

At that time Bath was known to those who did not care for it as 'the city where the young can't live and the old can't die'. Certainly many elderly couples lived there. During the blitz one such couple were going down from their bedrooms in their lodging house to the basement that passed for an air-raid shelter. Suddenly the wife turned back upstairs. 'What are you doing?' 'I've forgotten my teeth.' 'Oh come on, woman! They're dropping bombs not nuts.'

After my return from the Middle East, a short visit back to the Hydro at Matlock as an instructor. I had some captured German films that needed cutting and putting together into a short accompaniment to a lecture. The local cinema operator was happy to do the necessary work and we fell into conversation. 'I see you are showing *Brighton Rock*. Are you getting good audiences?' 'No,' he said in a broad Derbyshire accent, 'mostly officers from the Hydro. As a matter of fact the intellectual level of Matlock is not very high. You can always pack out with *Tarzan*.'

This short break with Ella provided a welcome interval between serious work in the Middle East and even more serious work at Montgomery's headquarters at St Paul's School in London, preparing for the invasion of Normandy. My boss was the brilliant Brigadier 'Bill' (now Sir Trevor) Williams – young at thirty three, who had headed Montgomery's intelligence staff in the Middle East. We therefore knew each other already.

This was my first experience of working with Americans, a people who were to play such an important part in my life, and very much so in the immediate future. Tactical bombing in support of the invasion was the joint task of the British Second Tactical Air Force and the Ninth US Army Air Force (a similar arrangement was made at strategic level). The headquarters were at the RAF base at Uxbridge in a country house environment. Under the chairmanship of Sir Arthur (later Lord) Tedder, Eisenhower's Deputy Supreme Commander, there were represented six armed services, three from each country. I was the number two to Brigadier Oxborrow, the BGS (Air) from Monty's headquarters.

The opportunities for tension between services and between countries were legion, but Tedder had a good sense of humour and Brigadier Ralph Stearley, the number three in the Ninth USAAF team, appointed himself the official defuser of arguments. At one moment of cross-purposes and confusion he weighed in with his deep, gravelly Texan accent – 'That reminds me of the Mexican War we had one time,' and went on, 'A Colonel was bringing his regiment up to the battle when he met the Commanding General and the Commanding General said to him, 'Just take your regiment in anywhere, Colonel. There's good fighting all along the line.'

An intriguing contrast arose between the British with their considerable skill and experience but not too many aircraft and the Americans with plenty of aircraft and crew but not so much experience. An elaborate Allied deception plan had been mounted before the invasion to persuade Rommel that the landings were going to come in the Pas de Calais rather than Normandy. This was largely successful, so it became important to destroy bridges over the River Seine to try to slow up German reinforcement of Normandy from the North. On Brigadier Oxborrow's behalf I approached the RAF, whose representative gave me the kind of pitying glance that the RAF reserve for the 'Brown Jobs'. 'My dear chap, it's not surprising, I suppose, but you really do not understand what would be involved. The chances of hitting one of those bridges from the kind of height that we would have to fly at are negligible and, of course, we would have to provide air cover for the attacking aircraft into the bargain. It's not on.'

Off I went to the USAAF who said, 'Sure, we'll have a go.' I reported this to the RAF who were derisive, and their derision increased as the Americans failed several times to get anywhere near a bridge. But eventually they hit one to good effect. This riled the RAF who then proceeded to hit other bridges with a smaller number of sorties.

A nice tailpiece about a particular bridge came from a member of the French Resistance. 'I am under the impression that you want the bridge at . . . destroyed, so I have blown it up myself.'

In spite of all the tensions at headquarters the two tactical airforces did a good job. The Luftwaffe were outnumbered and not very effective and though the difficult art of tactical attack in support of the Armies was not yet highly developed, and the inevitable 'foul-ups' occasionally occurred, the management of the tactical Air Forces came out on the credit side.

After the conclusive break-out at the end of the Battle of Normandy we received an exultant message from a member of the French Resistance 'Owing to the speed of the Allied advance I am having the greatest difficulty in keeping behind the enemy lines.'

As staff officers we had driven ourselves very hard, as indeed was only proper since, except on visits to Normandy, we did not share the same risks as the fighting troops. Partly from my nature, partly in my anxiety to do the best possible job, I had developed a sort of fierce efficiency. A similar characteristic, with its associated abruptness of manner, was shared by a number of people who had served previously under Montgomery. But I was more startled than I should have been to receive an emissary from Bill Williams, by then in Normandy, in the shape of his deputy, Colonel 'Joe' Ewart. He carried a letter saying that there was no further place for me at the Headquarters of 21 Army Group and that, therefore, I would not be going to France to join in the pursuit after the battle. The crucial sentence of the letter read 'I must have a happy ship.' He said that he had arranged for me to keep my rank of lieutenant colonel. From Joe's talk with me it was clear that, though Bill Williams' information was, to some extent, faulty, there was no chance of appealing. All I could do was to accept it and ask Joe to take back a letter trying to put the record a bit straighter.

The impact of this whole incident was reinforced by my number two who in later years became a friend. As I wrote my letter to Bill Williams he said with some relish 'You're finished!' The central fact was that I had become too intense and had paid inadequate attention to the sensibilities of those who worked for me and they had reacted against this. This was a mistake that I resolved never, if possible, to make again.

The curious limbo which resulted from this episode lasted for several months, except for a message from the War Office that they assumed I did not want to be posted to the Far East. At least I could share my penance with my wife, which was extremely pleasant as we had been apart for so long.

CHAPTER THREE

The World of Education

In December 1944 Sir Maurice Holmes, who had a few months still to run as Permanent Secretary to what was by then the Ministry of Education, rang me to say that the War Office had agreed to his proposal that I should return to that department. This came as a surprise and something of an embarrassment as the war was still in progress. But it was good to have the prospect of a job to do again. It was a change from watching from our flat north of Hyde Park a red flag being run up above the roof of Paddington station every time a VI flying bomb was approaching the area.

While all this wartime activity had been going on the officials of the Board of Education, evacuated to Bournmouth, had been engaged in what was probably the most distinguished piece of work ever done in that or its successor departments. Under the guidance of Sir Maurice Holmes as Permanent Secretary, they gave much thought to a comprehensive reform of the public educational system in England and Wales. They did it at a measured pace, not much disturbed by the exigencies of war, and they consulted a limited number of representatives of the Local Education Authorities, the teachers and the churches.

Apart from converting the Board of Education to a Ministry with increased powers, their reform rationalised the structure of the LEAs and reduced their number to 146. It also empowered them all to provide further education. It proposed the raising of the compulsory school age to fifteen and it provided for development plans to be drawn up by each LEA's as a blueprint for the future. And, most importantly, it spelt out the form of a settlement between the LEA's and the Churches. It also dealt with a variety of other subjects ranging from the training of teachers to special schools for handicapped children.

When Mr R. A. Butler was appointed President of the Board in 1941 Sir Maurice presented him with these proposals. In the words of Rab's autobiography he was 'on the whole much attracted by them' and he submitted them to the Prime Minister. Within twenty-four hours he received a flat rejection. Mr Churchill told him, in effect, to get on with his administrative work of keeping the schools going in the difficult conditions of wartime and to forget about elaborate plans for the future. Mr Butler boldly ignored this put-down and he and his officials began a series of complex negotiations with the representatives of interests outside central government. The most complex of all were the negotiations with the churches and to these Mr Butler's diplomatic skills made a decisive contribution. He was much assisted by his Labour Parliamentary Secretary Mr Chuter Ede, who had a close connection with the Free Churches. Eventually, in 1943, he emerged with his Education Bill, which was blessed by the Cabinet, were all the main political parties were represented, and passed into law, to applause from Mr Churchill. It was to lead to one of the greatest reforms which embodied the hopes for the Britain of the future.

The experienced reflective thought, the high standard of drafting and the skill in negotiation with familiar partners were characteristic of the Civil Service of the day. To translate the vision into reality at the same time as other reforms such as the creation of the National Health Service and the implementation of the Beveridge Report on Social Security and in the midst of the post-war scarcities of people, materials and money required rather different aptitudes, a faster pace and a more inter-departmental outlook.

The more aggressive behaviour towards Ministers and many departments on the part of Parliament and the media was yet to come. We were not yet in the era when every investigative media man's ambition was to uncover a new Watergate, but there was already some truth in the saying that in order to be a good journalist you have to distrust the Establishment.

To this rather new, more open world the mix of those who had shared hardships with their fellow men and women at home and those of us who had served in the forces was potentially a power for good. My own varied experience in the Services had been matched – or more than matched – by high fliers such as John Hunt (the future Secretary of the Cabinet) in the Navy, in the Western Approaches and the Far East; Frank Cooper (the future Permanent Under Secretary of State at the Ministry of Defence) in the RAF; Arnold France (later chairman of the board of Inland Revenue) in the Army in the Middle East; Pat Nairne (later the Permanent Secretary of the Department of Health and Social Security) who won an MC in the Seaforth Highlanders; and Peter Carey (my successor as Permanent Secretary of the Department of Trade and Industry) who spent two years behind the German lines in Yugoslavia.

This was not a generation to tolerate ignorance of the world outside Whitehall or to place undue emphasis on theory at the expense of practice.

Those in the Diplomatic Service were, of course, by definition attuned to conditions in other countries, but the *manner* in which they approached problems was influenced towards reality by experience in the armed services. From the Army, such people as Denis Greenhill and Michael Palliser, both later Heads of the Foreign & Commonwealth Office, and from the Navy, Antony Duff with a DSO, who became a Deputy Under Secretary of State and Oliver Wright with a DSC, who finished up as the British Ambassador in Washington.

At Education the successor to Sir Maurice Holmes would have an important influence on the style of the department. Both the leading candidates were extroverts. The 'inside' contender was Sir Robert Wood, fully capable of doing the job to good effect. But, partly because he was well into his fifties, he was passed over and had to be content with the substantial consolation prize of becoming the first Vice Chancellor of the new University of Southampton.

The man appointed was John Maud, like Oliver Franks a brilliant young wartime recruit from the University world to the services. He rose to the top of the Ministry of Food and was still only forty in 1945. He was, I suppose, the 'dashing cavalryman' of the post-war Service – very able, very personable – more of a public personality than some traditionalists cared for, but effective all the same in his relations with LEAs and teachers. His appointment more or less coincided with Labour's massive victory at the polls.

The new Minister was Ellen Wilkinson, whose courage and vigour had been much applauded when she was responsible for air-raid precautions at the Ministry of Home Security. She succeeded R. A. Butler, who had moved to be (briefly) Minister of Labour and Richard Law, who during the short-lived caretaker government before the general election doubled the jobs of Foreign Secretary and Minister of Education.

Dick Law was able to spend little time at Education and my chief benefit from him was a personal one. Ella and I, by then a bit desperate about somewhere fairly nice where we could afford to live, inherited his flat at Dolphin Square.

I became Principal Private Secretary to the three of them in rather quick succession. This appointment represents a most important stage in anyone's career. There is only one such job in each department. If the management has assessed performance and potential correctly and provided that the man or woman turns out to have enough staying power a Principal Private Secretary more often than not ultimately becomes a Permanent Secretary. The person concerned occupies a key position in the department linking the Secretary of State with his official colleagues and, of course, he must carry the complete confidence of both the Secretary of State and the Permanent Secretary. He or she is in for a couple of years or so of exceptionally hard work. The ability to deal acceptably with the outside world (Parliament, the department's 'constituency', the media) is of course vital. Rab, with his reputation high after the passage of the Education Act 1944, a family background in politics, a Rolls Royce of a brain and, perhaps, one weakness – an inclination to walk all round a problem taking, so to speak, a dozen snapshots in the time that

most people needed to take one, but an inability to make up his mind, to cut through the complexities of argument and to settle upon a firm decision.

Ellen arrived with the reputation of a revolutionary. Everyone remembered the Jarrow March in the 1930s to highlight the unemployment situation and, as I was to discover, she had a considerable reputation on the continent for her work in arranging for the escape of a number of prominent people from Nazi Germany. It was a surprise to find M. Leon Blum, a Prime Minister of France, calling on the British Minister of Education. But Ellen did not have the chance to be much of a revolutionary because Mr Attlee's policy in education was to implement the Butler Education Act. The rise to prominence of the comprehensive school issue was still many years away. She did have to her credit, however, the decision to go ahead with raising the compulsory school age from fourteen to fifteen.

In Cabinet the Chancellor of the Exchequer, Sir Stafford Cripps, naturally opposed it on the grounds that the country could not afford it, but with the Prime Minister on her side Ellen won the day. When the Cabinet minutes arrived I took them in to her and said, 'I don't suppose, Minister, that you will want to see these every time, but I thought you might like to read the official record of your item on the school leaving age.' I stood by her side while she read it. When she had finished she looked up and said, 'Well, Mr Part,' (she always called me Mr Part, never Antony) 'I never knew that I had attended such a cultured, well-phrased discussion.'

She taught me a lot about the Labour Party and the trades unions. She had become the national organiser of her own union, the Distributive and Allied Workers, at the age of 24 and on arriving by train in, I think, Birmingham to handle her first dispute had been greeted by the local trade union leader with 'Where's your father?'

Like Ella and me, she lived in Dolphin Square and on some evenings she would come across the square, put up her feet on our sofa and tell me what was wrong with me. On one such occasion we fell into a discussion about class-consciousness. I said, 'Well, I am not class-conscious.' Her Lancashire accent broadened. 'You, not class-conscious? My God! You should hear yourself talking to my driver.' After I had absorbed that punch I ventured a small counter-punch. 'I tell you one thing,' I said. 'I am not as class-conscious as my Minister.' 'Well no,' she said, 'that's true.'

In the face of shortages she got the Emergency Teachers Training Colleges for demobilised men and women underway and she fought for her department's share of scarce materials. She and John Maud made a lively pair. In some ways she was at her most effective in addressing large audiences and I gained a selfish benefit from hearing the differences in her style between talking to a small audience and facing a large one. Like a good actor, she would project her voice to the back of the hall, simplify the sentences, cut down the relative clauses and make sure that in the first few minutes she got a loud laugh or a lusty cheer.

When she went abroad her stature increased. Her most remarkable performance was her visit to Prague to open a British Film Festival there with a short speech before the showing of *Henry V* with Laurence Olivier as the King. At that stage of her life, Ellen was not in the best of health. She suffered from a mixture of asthma and bronchitis, which was distressing to see when it got bad.

She was ill when she boarded the small aircraft that flew us from Croydon via Germany to Prague, but she insisted on going. On arrival at our hotel she went straight to bed to get some rest before the evening show.

A doctor was organised and gave her what he called a 'bomb' injection to enable her to face the evening. About twenty minutes after the doctor had left the buzzer at the entrance of the suite sounded. I opened the door and there stood a distinguished-looking man with grey hair *en brosse* and the red button of a decoration in his buttonhole. 'Miss Wilkinson?' he enquired. 'Yes,' I said, 'May I know who you are?' 'I am the President's doctor.' For one awful moment I wondered who the first doctor had been and whether his treatment had been correct. But all was well. The first doctor's visit had been arranged by the interpreter and the President's doctor approved the treatment.

Come the evening and Ellen was still not at all well. But she would not give in. She was driven to the theatre and put in a room close by the side of the stage, where she could inhale something to give a little relief.

The show was opened by the Prague Symphony Orchestra playing an overture by Smetana. The curtains were then drawn across the stage and we carried Ellen from the side room along the side of the stage to the prompter's corner. The orchestra, still then in place, were moved, some of them to tears, by her courage. The audience waited for her appearance. There stood a lonely microphone centre-stage in front. She insisted on making her public appearance unaided. This small figure, five feet tall, with her red hair and her long apple-green evening dress, walked alone valiantly to the microphone. She made a speech lasting three minutes, to great applause. She walked steadily back to the prompter's corner – and collapsed. We took her back into the side room where a doctor and helpful equipment were waiting, and after a time that seemed unbearably long she was transported back to the hotel. It may have been foolhardy, but it matched the splendour of the occasion. In spite of all, she had done what she came to Prague to do.

By this time the work of the Civil Service had changed radically since before the war. In the thirties the Service was relatively small, public expenditure was rigorously limited, the media were not particularly intrusive (except, of course, on major matters such as Anglo-German relations), television was in its infancy and, perhaps most important of all, the ideal of the Tories, who had been in power for most of the time between the wars, was that government should be minimal.

Now, in 1946, the comprehensive web of wartime controls was reinforced by the Labour Government's desire for more central planning. To these were added the competing claims on a weak economy of the repairing of the war damage and of the various major social reforms worked out in wartime. All this led to the continuation of rationing (some of it until 1953) and, therefore, continued contact between the electorate and the officials responsible for the day-to-day work, more stringent controls of expenditure by public bodies and, within government, much inter-departmental infighting for a 'fair' share of what was going in the way of resources.

The size of the Civil Service increased from 150,000 in 1938 to 450,000 in 1946 and thus to a potential source of future conflict between departments and the interests outside government.

For some departments – though not Education – the international dimension had grown significantly, particularly in the economic sphere, and a distinction became increasingly apparent between the ethos of those Departments, such as the Board of Trade, that had strong and regular contacts with other countries, and those, such as the Home Office and the Ministry of Health, that were concerned almost solely with home affairs. In this second group there was less of an automatic guarantee that the outlook would be broad and outgoing or, to put it another way, the officials in those departments had to make a special effort to see that introspection was avoided. This was a contribution which the generation of civil servants who had served in the forces was well suited to reinforce.

Opportunity cut my time as a Private Secretary to eighteen months. Rather suddenly appointment as the Head of Buildings and Priority Branch came along. This apparently pedestrian post led, in the event, to one of the most exciting and stimulating jobs that any civil servant could have. It also led directly to a marvellous year in the United States in 1950–1.

The promotion was, of course, welcome but it was sad to leave Ellen Wilkinson who was, alas, overwhelmed by her asthma and bronchitis a few months later.

Her successor, Mr George Tomlinson, was in a different way a most interesting character. Unlike Ellen, who had a university degree, poverty had obliged him to leave school as soon as the law allowed. Like many such people, he felt this disadvantage strongly and was determined to do his bit to see that educational opportunity for everyone improved. He went into local government and took an increasingly informed interest in educational administration. On Ellen's death he reached the peak of his ambition when he was appointed to succeed her.

He was a great observer of human nature. The memorial service for Ellen was attended by the whole Cabinet. The service included the hymn which finishes:

> Oh that we now might grasp our guide
> Oh that the lead were given
> Let Jordan's narrow waves divide
> And land us safe in heaven!

Coming out of the church with John Maud the Minister remarked in his slow Lancashire tones, 'And when we got to last verse I looked round at Cabinet and I thought "It will be a grave disappointment to them if the Lord takes them at their word."'

His insight made him a most effective man at a meeting. It was always said that when he and Mr Aneurin Bevan had an argument he won. This was because Mr Bevan, having a combative mind, was always thinking how he could quickly demolish his opponent, whereas Mr Tomlinson would bide his time and then land a knock-out blow. He was also a wily tactician. Each year the Association of Education Committees came to the Minister to present to him the resolutions which they had passed at their annual conference. On one occasion the resolutions included, as Item 5, one on denominational education, a subject in which Mr Tomlinson was not too expert. Officials spent quite some time briefing him before the deputation but were not confident that he had mastered the complexities.

The deputation was led by a local authority spokesman whom he knew quite well. Official breaths were held as the discussion on Item 4 drew to a close. 'Now Jim,' said the Minister, 'we come to Item 5. You know and I know that the Association has to pass a resolution of this kind every year and we are all quite familiar with the arguments. Shall we move on to Item 6?' It was like a sucker-punch and by the time the leader of the deputation had got his breath the discussion on Item 6 had started.

His folksy sense of humour stood him in good stead when he visited schools and colleges. Opening a new wing of a teachers training college for girls he said, 'You have a wonderful college here, girls. The only trouble is that the moment you have finished your training many of you get married. I have been looking into the marriage rates of different types of student and do you know what I find? I find that the quickest to get married are the domestic science students, then come the speech therapists. Do you know what I conclude from that? I conclude that though the quickest way to a man's heart may be through his stomach if that fails you can always talk him into it.'

So far as policy goes he was not a Labour theorist. He represented himself as a man with strong sympathy for the underdog, anxious to get on with a practical job in very difficult circumstances; and he did this to great effect. This very much included school building.

Post-war building was a rat-race between government departments. Housing had priority to make good the wartime damage, to provide for the men and women returning from the forces and to make a start on the ring of new towns around London, such as Crawley, Harlow and Stevenage, recommended by Professor Abercrombie. For schools the centre of the stage was held by building for the raising of the school leaving age. This was to be done by Nissen huts, which were unsightly and of temporary construction.

The government appreciated too late that much new housing, particularly in the new towns, would require new schools and that, following such large scale demobilisation a large number of babies were likely to be born. All this against the background that enemy air attacks had damaged one school in every four in England and Wales and, indeed, destroyed a good number of them. As things turned out the appropriate target for the period between 1947 and 1952 was to get one thousand new schools completed and to have a further one thousand under construction. This represented a considerable challenge to the LEAs and the Ministry.

There was a shortage of technically qualified manpower, from architects to building craftsmen, particularly bricklayers. The Ministry would have to fight hard for their allocations of scarce materials; the amount of timber allocated by the Materials Committee for School Building in England and Wales for a year was no more than the amount allowed over the same period to one glass manufacturer for packing his exports. The Ministry would also need arrangements co-ordinated with the Regional Officers of the Ministry of Works so that the necessary 'starting dates' for building could be obtained to time. Finally, the administrative procedures at both Ministry and LEA level were too slow to match the pace required. It was clear that fabrication of components off the site would need to play a substantial part; otherwise the very large number of school places required could never be provided. There was some talk of Nissen huts and other temporary buildings; but such buildings on so big a scale would have been visually unacceptable and, on account of their short life, not cost-effective either.

Meanwhile, just to make life more difficult, there had been in progress since 1943 a sustained argument between two powerful factions about the most suitable horizontal dimensional basis for industrialised building for schools. One appeared, at first sight, to be the cheaper. The other gave the designer much more freedom to arrange the accommodation with greater imagination so as to accord with the newer teaching methods. The problem was made no easier by the fact that of the two Deputy Secretaries (the most senior officials under Sir John Maud) one favoured the first solution, the other the second. But on one thing both agreed and so did the Minister and John Maud. The Ministry should not cause to be produced anything like 'National Schools' of various sizes which would be based on standard plans – like pre-fabricated houses but of course larger.

A survey of this rather unsatisfactory scene brought one thought quickly to mind. The various regulations, controls and timetables did not make practical sense for the LEAs. The Ministry must create a more satisfactory framework so as to enable the LEAs to perform more efficiently.

School building was a good example of one of the most characteristic functions of civil servants. In a very great deal of their work it is their task, with the approval of Ministers, to be realistic but imaginative scene-setters so as to enable the prime-movers, whether they be public bodies or private organisations, to do their job to the best and, in the case of industry, the most profitable advantage. These arrangements would have to be flexible enough to cover both the immediate emergency and later developments. The key to success seemed to be to settle for each LEA an itemised list of major projects permitted to be started on the site in a particular year. When the system had got underway we would also aim to approve for each Authority seventy per cent of a programme for the following year. By this means we would establish a sort of 'assembly line technique' so that at any one time there would be an adequate volume of proposals at each stage.

We aimed to announce as soon as possible the arrangements for compiling the first 'Operational Programme', a title deliberately chosen for its military overtones. Except for a minority who were not used to committing themselves for a year ahead, the LEAs were not too hard to convince because such a programme would clearly be to their advantage. One of its essential features had to be that a place in a programme would guarantee that all the controls operated by government would follow automatically, provided that the LEA had done its job properly. These controls were technical and financial approval of plans, rations of steel and timber, a general permit to use other building materials, a starting date from the appropriate Regional Officer of the Ministry of Works (the sponsoring department for the construction industry) and approval of the necessary loan.

Our self-imposed timetable required that we complete negotiations in Whitehall within one month with all the government interests involved, from the Treasury, through the Ministry of Works and the Public Works Loan Board to, by no means the easiest, the other interests in the Ministry of Education such as Schools Branch, Architects Branch and Finance Branch.

We ran into three problems. The first was that the existing arrangements required the approval of each project by the Ministry of Education at both sketch-plan and final plans stage; an internal working party had recently recommended cutting out approval at sketch-plan stage, but we felt that that was the more important step for the Ministry to vet as it fixed the controlling parameters for each project. The local authority could be trusted to carry on from there. Fortunately, the senior official who had chaired the working party gave way with good grace when he saw the shape of the package as a whole.

The second problem was that the PWLB, who were – deliberately – independent of government, declined to guarantee loan approval in advance. But they allowed us to give the LEAs to understand that they could normally expect approval. And the PWLB honoured this undertaking.

The third – and most teasing – problem was that scarce materials were allocated only for three months ahead. As this arrangement held good for all government departments and all materials, the (rather senior) officials concerned could not be convinced that they should make an exception for the Ministry of Education in respect of steel and timber, and we had no reason to think that pressure at Ministerial or Permanent Secretary level would be more effective. In the end we concluded that, so long as the annual school building programme which we wanted to approve coincided broadly in size with the sum of the quarterly allocations likely to be available we should be able to get by. This worked all right for every LEA except Hertfordshire, whose innovatory methods (which ultimately became more influential than those of any other LEA) required them to commit themselves to orders to their suppliers of steel twelve months ahead. However, because they were the only LEA with this problem we were able to accommodate them.

The arrangements for the operational programme were announced, as planned, within the month, and the response from the LEAs, whose representatives had been included in our consultations, was good. One more administrative innovation was required. It was important to the success of this and later programmes that the approvals, particularly in the regions, should not only be announced as guaranteed but that they should actually be forthcoming in practice. Otherwise confidence in the whole machinery would be impaired.

We were allowed to recruit as temporary civil servants a Regional Priority Officer for each of the regions. He was to be a trouble-shooter, whose job would be to sort out on the spot any delays in the supply of materials and labour and, in particular, to liaise between the LEAs and the regional officers of the Ministry of Works. Not surprisingly, these jobs turned out to be attractive to senior regular officers who had retired at the end of the war, and this remarkable group of men brought fresh air into the whole operation. They suited us and we suited them. In terms of seniority they were headed by a major-general and included the former captain of the Eastern Fleet and a group captain from the RAF. The others were majors or above. There was only one civilian and he was an experienced progress-chaser from the Admiralty.

The military element was completed by the appointment as Administrative Officers at headquarters of two former regular army officers, one of whom had been the Brigadier in charge of administration and supplies at the headquarters in which I had served in the desert. All these senior men were very tolerant of their youthful boss and, though this military enclave was not approved of by everyone in the Ministry, we had fun as well as job satisfaction. The RPOs contributed significantly to the practical success of the school building programme.

The developments in Hertfordshire imparted an invaluable dimension to the whole operation. The Chief Education Officer, John (later Sir John) Newsom was very intelligent and full of ideas about the way education should develop. He was also gregarious and his relationship with the teachers was good. He was not the most methodical of men, but his Deputy, Sidney Broad, was a first class administrator.

The County Architect, C. H. Aslin, was a wise, elderly man who gathered about him the most talented group of young architects to be found, if not anywhere in the country, then certainly in educational building. Aslin's Deputy, Stirrat Johnson-Marshall, with David Medd and his wife Mary (whose professional name was Crowley), Anthony Pott and the quantity surveyor Jim Nisbet became names to conjure with as the years went by. Yet they were not seekers after personal publicity; indeed, most of them shunned it.

This stimulating team had both the challenge and the opportunity of one of the largest school building programmes in the country. Their most important contribution was their skill at drawing from teachers and officials alike ideas on educational methods and activities. They said, for example, 'Don't please tell us about the number of rooms that you want and their dimensions. We would like to know what you propose should be *done* in the teaching areas and the communal spaces.' In the primary schools they discovered that all classrooms should not necessarily be of a uniform size or shape and that the children no longer sat in serried ranks but worked in much smaller groups of, say, five or six, each group not always doing the same thing. They also learnt that the traditional design of the communal spaces was often neither suitable nor economical. Finally, they worked out for themselves that, in primary schools at least, corridors could be cut to a minimum.

Hertfordshire were not the first or the only authority to think about education in this way. But in those early post-war days they carried much further than anyone else the close collaboration between educators and architects. In architectural design they were followers of Walter Gropius and the Bauhaus School. This involved establishing function as the guiding principle of design and arranging for as many components as possible to be fabricated off the site and making their erection as simple as could be managed. They were ingenious in devising, in close collaboration with a manufacturer, Hills of West Bromwich, a kind of meccano set of light steel components which could be put together in a wide variety of ways with a clever mixture of imagination and economy. They did the same for glass, roofing and walling materials. In one extreme case they were able to get a whole school built by only twelve men.

This resulted in flat roofs (which were anathema to some people) and, in the early stages, a rather utilitarian appearance. But they made ingenious use of such things as colour, murals and sculpture. People of the calibre of Henry Moore, George Ehrlich and Barbara Hepworth were prepared to accept commissions at manageable prices. (Later the Ministry formally announced that up to one per cent of the approved expenditure on a new school building could be devoted to works of art.)

These innovations extended to the system of heating and ventilation, toilets, washbasins and, in later years, to school furniture and to the invention of a scientific colour code, which was accepted by architects and manufacturers, to ensure greater efficiency of design and more accurate standards of manufacture. It was their work on structure that first brought them into close contact with those of us who were responsible for the administration of school buildings.

The authority's first annual programme consisted of a dozen new schools. Their Meccano-set approach enabled them – indeed required them for reasons of economy – to assure the steel component manufacturer of a particular volume of business in the year ahead. It was, incidentally, this approach, eventually introduced into the Ministry when these same architects later joined its staff, that ensured that in the whole post-war history of school building – lasting twenty or thirty years – not a penny of the taxpayers' or ratepayers' money was spent on grants to manufacturers for development. They were expected to rely, as they did, on the existence of annual building programmes as a near-guarantee that they could cover their development costs if their products were good.

In making their case to the Ministry in 1946 for the necessary steel permits the Hertfordshire architects explained in detail their approach to structural design. They convinced us that their 'square grid' system not only allowed the designer much greater flexibility but also enabled him to economise on corridors or even sometimes to dispense with them altogether. This approach was vital to the philosophy and practical application of their ideas about design. In nearly all cases it was cheaper than the rival one-directional bay system (a row of classrooms with a corridor alongside and other corridors to link the remaining spaces to the classrooms).

At this early stage we at the Ministry were concerned almost solely with the problems that this approach involved in connection with the issue of approvals for the use of a given amount of steel for a programme of starts stretching over a year. But the merits of the approach stuck in our minds and in the minds of the HMIs concerned with, as will be seen, tremendously important results.

With the operational programme (for a single year) underway, the principle of an annual succession of short-term programmes in place, with reserve programmes (seventy per cent of their associated short-term programme) accepted as a technique, the prospect of housing the one million extra primary school children resulting from the post-war 'bulge in the birthrate' was greatly improved.

Two more pieces remained to be put in place in the administrative jigsaw: the organisation of the Ministry for handling school building and the control of costs. Both gave rise to constructive developments that were to exert a major influence on the school building process.

The first arose from the retirement of Jackman, the Ministry's Chief Architect, in 1948. A well-respected modest man, his lowly grading as a Principal – the first rank above the training grade of Assistant Principal – prevented him from exerting any very substantial influence within the Ministry, let alone outside it. His successor needed to be someone with the ability and the creativeness to assess and inspire future developments in design and building practice and to have at the same time a personality that would be acceptable both within the Ministry and outside it.

A selection board was held under the chairmanship of Sir John Maud and included among the candidates was Stirrat Johnson-Marshall. He was what might be called a practical visionary. Both aspects of this description were already embodied in Hertfordshire's post-war performance. At the same time he had an almost passionate attachment to the concept of personal anonymity in public: he was very much a team man.

He was clearly the outstanding candidate and his proposal for the formation in the ministry of a development group met with a ready response from the selection board. But his insistence that the development group should not only develop approaches and solutions but apply them in practice by building a few schools was clearly going to cause us no end of trouble with the LEAs, the architectural profession and, perhaps, the teachers too.

However, the concept was so clearly right, provided that it could be implemented with adequate attention to external sensibilities, that we accepted the challenge, appointed him and spent the six months before his arrival negotiating with the outside interests concerned for their acceptance and, if possible, their support. We emphasised that the development group would build only a few schools in order to try out new educational and technical ideas and that they would build them for the LEAs concerned on exactly the same terms as a private architect would.

Looking back it seems incredible that the negotiations were so tough and prolonged. But the first antagonistic reaction of the LEAs emphasised the delicacy of the balance between central and local government that had been enshrined in the Butler Act of 1944, and the fact that the RIBA thought it necessary to make representations at a high level in the Ministry illustrated their fears, which were quite unfounded, of government interference in their professional freedom of design. However, all was well in the end and we felt that there must be more in common between the Home Civil Service and the Diplomatic Service than we had at first supposed!

The final manoeuvres took place inside the Ministry. The proposal to combine the Buildings & Priority Branch with the Architects Branch was fairly easily agreed; but my proposal that the Chief Architect should be head of the Branch with me as his deputy was violently opposed by the First Division Association (the trade union of the Civil Service administrators), and after some rather delicate footwork the concept of joint heads of an Architects and Building Branch was adopted. This early example of a team of mixed skills (which also included an HMI and later a quantity surveyor) depended, of course, on good relations between Stirrat Johnson-Marshall and me, but there was no problem about that. We embarked upon a friendship that lasted until his death some thirty years later.

Up to this stage Ministerial approval had been sought when necessary, but for the most part John Maud's authority was sufficient. On the next point Ministers were inescapably involved. It concerned the control of costs and the economic crisis of 1949.

Whatever else we had done well we had not done well on the control of costs. This was partly because we had given priority to getting a co-ordinated operation effectively underway on a large scale and partly because, on account of the massive inflation in the interval, there was no sensible basis on which to compare post-war costs with the closely controlled pre-war costs, though an internal

Ministry review suggested that costs had risen between two and three times since the 1930s and that eighty per cent of the rise was due to increased costs of building materials and labour and twenty per cent to the higher standards embodied in the Ministry's post-war building regulations. Finally, there was not yet enough evidence to assess the implications of the comparative costs of different LEAs. The variations were very great: in Yorkshire the cost per child of a new primary school in Doncaster and Huddersfield was around £75 whereas the equivalent figure for Leeds was £240.

So we were vulnerable – and the more so because the Ministry of Health had just completed a very efficient report on the costs of house building. We had, however, been doing some research within the Ministry and we were ready with an announcement to coincide with the Prime Minister's statement on the economic crisis following the revaluation of the dollar against the pound from $4.03 to $2.80. This statement, in which the Minister (then Mr Tomlinson) and the Permanent Secretary had, of course, been heavily involved, set new indicative limits on the number of square feet per pupil to be allowed in primary and secondary schools. Compared with 1949 there was to be a reduction overall of 12½ per cent in the cost per place with the reduction of a further 12½ per cent in 1951 continuing on at that level to 1952.

The savings achieved were very substantial. Between January 1950 and the third quarter of 1952 over 550,000 new school places were due to be started in major projects, even on the post-war policy of limiting new projects to 'roofs over heads'. Against this challenging background Johnson-Marshall introduced two valuable innovations. The first was the publication by the Ministry of 'Building Bulletins', the first being on the design of primary schools. They included educational ideas culled from HMIs and, through HMIs, from the LEAs and teachers, and they translated these into approaches to design.

In order to forestall any (mistaken) criticism that the Ministry were trying to impose detailed solutions on the LEAs, we made it crystal clear that the Building Bulletins were advisory only and that Ministry approval of a major project would certainly not be subject to the incorporation of these ideas. In the end, between

1949 and 1964, twenty three such Bulletins were published. They constitute a remarkable and stimulating record of progressive and practical ideas on school building over those fifteen years.

Johnson-Marshall's other vitally important move was to import – again from Hertfordshire – Jim Nisbet, a talented young quantity surveyor, who, as the years went by, was to contribute more than anyone else to getting value for money in school building. The traditional method of quantity surveying estimated the cost of the whole building well enough, but did little to help the architects to be conscious of where the money was going. Some spent excessively on expensive service ducts under corridors, some spent too much on the roof; and nobody knew the cost of a wall which consisted partly of glass and partly of other materials.

Nisbet developed a form of analysis which displayed the cost of the various elements in the building and developed this later into 'cost planning' which enabled the architect to set himself targets for the design of the various component parts of a building.

With the development of annual building programmes, the co-ordination of controls and their implementation on the ground, the arrival of Johnson-Marshall and his colleagues, the formation of the development group, the imposition of cost limits related to post-war experience and the importation of Jim Nisbet, the school building operation was 'up and running'. By 1952 the required 1000 new schools had been completed and rather more than the further 1000 were under construction.

It was an exciting experience. Johnson-Marshall was a stimulating leader whose beliefs were firmer than his manner suggested. He never wrote anything down, which alone differentiated him from traditional civil servants. He had twenty new ideas a day and one of the most important functions of the administrative joint-head of the Branch was to identify the good one.

The reputation of the British school building operation spread to the United States where it was admired by a number of leading American architects, and in 1960 Sir David Eccles, then the Minister of Education for the second time, made the enlightened gesture of putting up £30,000 to enable a small British school to be designed and built at the prestigious Milan Triennale. It was the joint work of architects from Nottinghamshire, who had pioneered a particular technique of pre-fabrication, and of others from the Ministry. It won the *Gran premio con menzione speciale*. This was a splendid manifestation of the continued vitality of the British school-building operation.

The whole history of this operation is admirably and meticulously surveyed, with the help of access to government papers, by Stuart Maclure, the former editor of the Times Educational Supplement, in a book entitled *Educational Development – School Building – Aspects of Public Policy 1945/73*. (Published as a tribute to the late Sir John Newson by Longmans, of which he was a director).

There was, however, no room for complacency. A study by Doctor (later Dame) Kathleen Ollerenshaw, who has been for many years a leading figure in educational administration in Manchester, showed that in 1954 three-quarters of a million of children (out of a total of over six million) were in schools built before the Education Act of 1870, and two million more in buildings put up before 1903.

From our post-war building programme we learnt two important lessons of more general application. The first was that if you are going to get involved in a continuing operation with a number of different organisations it greatly increases your chances of success if you have made friends with the key people in these organisations. A good instance in our case was Dr W. P. (later Lord) Alexander, the powerful Secretary of the Association of Education Committees. For example, his conversion to the proposal that the Development Group should be allowed to build a few schools was crucial to our success, for we knew that the LEAs would follow his lead. The second lesson was that you should respect the balance of power between you and your various partners and should try to ensure, so far as is practicable, that everyone should gain *some* advantage from the operation.

All this gave rise to the need for a great many personal contacts and a great deal of travelling. One selfish benefit was getting to know England and Wales as a whole much better than I had had a chance to before. For example, I had the good fortune to enter Wales for the first time not by the traditional route through Cardiff and the coalfields with an uninformed sense of countryside to the north, but to enter via the north coast and work southwards through that lovely scenery so that the coalfields appeared suddenly as black but minor gashes on the landscape.

Now, in 1950, travel beckoned still further afield. John Maud suggested that I apply for a Commonwealth Fund Fellowship from the Harkness Foundation. Among the early Fellows were Alastair Cooke, Geoffrey Crowther and Eric Linklater. So the standard was challenging. However, as up to five places were reserved each year for civil servants, the competition was not in practice too severe. Unlike the post-graduate academics who accounted for the great majority of the Fellowship, we did not have to be at a university all the time until the long summer vacation allowed opportunity for travel. But one did have to propose a subject and to write a substantial report for the whole Fellowship at the end. I chose educational building and, fortunately as it turned out, took with me a number of slides of our recent efforts in Britain.

In September Ella and I left Southampton as cabin-class passengers on the first *Queen Elizabeth*. We were stunned and – perhaps rather pompously – shocked by the amount and variety of food that was provided. We must have eaten about a month's worth of a British butter ration in less than a week.

We hit – or rather were hit by – the equinoctial gales. In those days there were no stabilisers, so the ship pitched atrociously. For Sunday morning service we were at first puzzled that there were no chairs, but the crew knew what they were doing. The congregation stood in fairly close-up rows. When the bows of the great ship went down we could see nothing but the sea ahead and when they went up we could see nothing but the cloudy sky. We moved as a single mass several steps forward during the first process and a similar number of steps back during the second, singing all the while 'For those in peril on the sea'.

Eventually, on a fine autumn morning, the Statue of Liberty and the famous silhouette of Manhatten Island, increasingly impressive as we approached. And then the American experience, starting with the lesson that in a hotel in the USA you must always lock your bedroom door. We failed to do so once in Michigan and were told off by the house detective, and once in Atlanta Ella woke up to find an intruder trying to rifle her handbag.

From our arrival onwards we were overwhelmed by hospitality in thirty or more states of the Union. First we reported to Harvard, where Professor Homer Anderson, a distinguished former Schools Superintendent of Denver, briefed me on the American educational system and the great variety of American approaches to school building. Through his kindness and that of Dr. Walter Cocking in New York, editor of the influential magazine *The School Executive*, we were hooked into a most helpful network of educators and architects throughout the US. We were doubly fortunate to have an introduction from John Maud to an American contemporary of his when he spent a year at Harvard, a descendant of an old and distinguished New England family. James Lawrence, an architect of sensibility, lived in an elegant country house just outside Boston, which he had designed as a wedding present for his beautiful wife Martina.

It quickly became apparent that to be a civil servant in the United States was not at all the same thing as to be in the same occupation in Britain. Because most of the senior members of an American government department change with a change of government, there is almost no equivalent of the British administrative class and when civil servants do reach a fairly senior rank they tend to be at least fifty years old. On top of that a career in the public service did not rank high in American esteem. Business of some kind was much more attractive. So they regarded me as a rather curious phenomenon and sometimes gave the impression that they wanted to touch me to see if I was real. But they were very friendly and only too ready to take time to show me round their schools.

The architects, on the other hand, were nearly all in private practice. The great Walter Gropius took me round parts of Harvard and explained how in the lay-out of the courtyards and their relationship to each other he had deliberately copied Oxford and Cambridge. Five years later, when James Lawrence got me back to give an illustrated talk to the New England Chapter of the American Institute of Architects, Gropius turned up to see the colour slides of the post-war British schools. Afterwards he came over to me and set his seal of approval on the British architects' work. In his gruff voice, with his still strong German accent, he spoke a single sentence: 'I am glad I came.' It was a pleasure to report this back to Stirrat Johnson-Marshall and his colleagues.

The other architects that we met were legion. Indeed, we met many of them when we were invited to attend the annual convention of the American Association of School Administrators at Atlantic City. It was our first experience of American razzamatazz on a big scale and General George Marshall made the key-note speech to an audience of several thousand.

Translation from one milieu to another was not always as quick as it might have been. One day at Atlantic City I wore my old Harrovian tie. A new acquaintance greeted me with 'Hi, Tony, I didn't know you were a member of the Larchmont Yacht Club.' 'Ignorant fellow' I thought, unreasonably, at the time. I later discovered that the Larchmont Yacht Club in New York State was a far more select organisation than Harrow School.

We ran into American politics. In New York we had stayed for most of the time with a generous lady whom we had met on the *Queen Elizabeth*. On the day when two Puerto Ricans tried to assassinate President Truman we were going back into her apartment block when we met the janitor. I said politely, 'I hear someone has tried to shoot the President.' 'Yeah,' he said, 'too bad they missed!' Another political aside came from a man whom we met in a drugstore in Washington. We were under the mistaken impression that Roosevelt was as much of a hero in the US as he had been in Britain during the war. It was clear that our friend didn't think so. But it was also clear that he wished to be polite to the two young British visitors. He summed up judiciously. 'No,' he said, 'I don't believe I could ever put my trust in a man who uses a cigarette holder.'

The third political encounter was of a much more serious nature. A woman friend of my mother's had given us an introduction to a couple in Washington. 'Do contact Aileen,' her mother said, 'I'm sure she will invite you over for a drink.' Which she did. Soon her lodger arrived. He worked in the British Embassy and his name was Guy Burgess. The Korean War was in progress and he expressed very unpatriotic views on the subject. He got quite drunk and his views became more emphatic. I was very annoyed and got as near to losing my temper as seemed acceptable in a friend's house. It crossed my mind that I should report this conversation to the Ambassador (Oliver Franks, as it happened) on whom I was due to call. But I thought – mistakenly – that that would be rather officious and that, in any case, Burgess must have expressed the same views often enough to his colleagues.

Tempers had cooled a bit and we were on the point of leaving when Aileen's husband arrived home having had to work late at the Embassy. His name was Kim Philby.

Christmas found us in Chicago in a modest hotel at the northern end of the Windy City. And windy it certainly was. Cold too – a temperature on one day of minus fifteen degrees fahrenheit (the coldest that I have ever experienced) with the wind whipping the frozen water at the lakeside into barbaric shapes.

We were down to our last twenty five dollars as my monthly pay cheque was late in arriving from England. A telephone call from Lawrence Perkins, like his father one of America's leading school architects, whom I had met at a lunch party in New York. A big, tall man, then about forty, with a domed head, already rather bald, and an idiosyncratic, rather throw-away self-depreciatingly humorous way of talking. Larry invited Ella and me to lunch with him and his family on Christmas Day at their roomy home, built by his father, at Evanston – a well-to-do suburb a few miles north of our hotel. We spent most of our remaining dollars on a present for the four children (credit cards had not yet been invented) and gladly enjoyed the hospitality on what would otherwise have been a rather lonely day. It was the start of a warm friendship which has lasted ever since.

Larry and his firm, Perkins & Will, designed many schools. The most rewarding, for an architect, were in the suburbs outside the big cities, for education in the United States is very locally controlled and the people in the suburbs could afford to pay much more than those in less fortunate circumstances. The control was so local that in 1950 there were in the United States 90,000 School Boards. So the only School Boards comparable in size with the

British LEAs were those in the large cities such as Chicago, Los Angeles, Boston and New York. The Boards operated under the suzerainty of a State Department of Education, which laid down a framework of controls and provided some money. In school building the most intelligent and imaginative State Departments were Michigan and California. As a matter of principle the federal government was kept out of almost everything except a few special programmes of aid such as money for school meals.

Larry's father had been responsible for the design of the Crow Island Elementary School near Chicago, a pioneering adventure into informality and lightness for small children. Larry continued the tradition. Perhaps not surprisingly because of the similarities of approach, he was much taken with the post-war British designs, which were quite unlike the pseudo-Tudor or Gothic which most American architects seem to have expected, and the exchange of views was stimulating and congenial.

Fortunately for us the Chicago Department of Education, led by Dr Herold Hunt, a tough, experienced administrator, also took a kindly interest in us, including an invitation to Herold's home. It was the time when the gadget had been invented that you hold in your hand to change the TV channels without going anywhere near the set. Lounging in his armchair, he was showing it off to us. 'Herold,' I said, 'what do you do if the gadget doesn't work?' 'Simple,' he said, 'I call for my wife to change the channel.'

This piece of male chauvinism (not seriously meant, of course) was quite uncharacteristic of the matriarchal society that America has been – at least in modern times. There are various theories about the reason for this. Some believe that, as a result of traditions going back to the prairie wagon days, the American woman's home was *her* responsibility and *her* 'castle' to a much greater extent than in Europe, but I think it has much to do with the fact that in the United States boys are taught by women to a much later age than they usually are in Britain. Though the Commonwealth Fund demurred at the 'matriarchal society' reference in my report, it is an impression shared by all my British friends.

Through Herold's kindness we were invited to the annual dinner of the Chicago Teachers' Association. It was a large and cheerful affair and we sat at a round table immediately below the centre of the long raised top table. As the occupants of the top table made their entrance in single file the band played 'The gang's all here'. We were then invited to put our hands on our neighbour's shoulders, sway from right to left and back again, singing as we did so a little song, the words of which were on a card in front of us. When it was over, Ella's American neighbour asked her 'Do you do this kind of thing in England?' To her great credit she replied 'Not on water!'

Unlike today, Chicago was then very isolationist and conscious of the growing power of the 'Land of the Free'. The lady anthropologist who was the Guest of Honour made a powerful speech ending with this passage: 'Two thousand years ago the proudest boast that a man could make was "I am a Roman citizen". I suppose that a hundred years ago the proudest boast was "I am a British citizen". But today (and her voice deepened to a fine contralto) – 'the future is to America, and we in the United States know something that neither the Romans nor the British ever knew' (crescendo) 'that with power goes responsibility'. She sat down to massive applause from several hundred people. Protest would have been inappropriate.

The Americans were always quick to comment on the English accent: often favourably, but on occasion not. One of the other Civil Service Fellows went into a drugstore in Chicago and ordered what I think must have sounded like 'tomahto juice'. The girl behind the counter made some remark to her boss which my friend didn't hear, but he did hear the boss's reply. 'Yeah', he said 'and if Jesus Christ Himself comes in you serve Him too.'

Back then through the snow and ice (not much fun in places for a relatively inexperienced driver) via school visits and school building meetings in the Middle West to Washington. There we met at dinner Denis and Angela Greenhill (now Lord and Lady Greenhill of Harrow) who were serving at the Embassy at that time. In later life, when he was the Permanent Head of the Foreign and Commonwealth Office and I was the Permanent Secretary of the Department of Trade and Industry, we saw a great deal of each other and this close friendship has lasted right through our careers in the public service and the ten years or more of our business lives after retirement from the Service. So this first encounter in Washington in the spring of 1951 was a bonus for Ella and me.

Then on south in the early spring to Georgia. This was when the large size of the United States began to make its impact, for we had started upon a sweep which was to take us by road down to New Orleans, across Texas and Arizona, up the west coast from Los Angeles to Seattle and then back east via Denver and Chicago to Boston in early August. With some exceptions we lived a 'motel and drugstore' kind of life.

Arrival in Georgia in the early spring, with the peach trees in flower against the bright red soil, brought an echo of earlier days. We had reserved a cheap room at the rather imposing Biltmore Hotel in Atlanta and were shown up to a room which was little short of a suite. Obviously a misunderstanding, to be corrected immediately. The manager said, 'No, that is not the correct rate for that room, but I want to tell you something. During the war I was in the United States Army and I was stationed for a long time in London during the bombing and the rationing, and I received such generous hospitality from your British families that I thought it would be a nice thing to put you and your wife in that room on this occasion.'

I was naturally much moved by that, but there was to be a further gesture of generosity. The next morning I came down early for breakfast, on my own, into the hotel foyer where newspapers and other things were being sold. Behind the counter was a really beautiful blonde and I have remembered to this day the words that she greeted me with: 'Good morning,' she said in a cheerful tone. 'What can I do for you, honey?' I was very tempted to tell her.

Quickly on then to Macon some hundred miles south of Atlanta, and the start of another lifelong friendship with McKibben Lane – an attorney, who was in his spare time, chairman of the local Board of Education, his wife Linda, a Southern belle if there ever was one, and their family.

The schools in Macon were segregated by colour in those days, as they were everywhere else in the South. The lower standards of the schools for blacks were fairly evident. Macon was also in the Bible Belt and going to church on Sunday was as much part of the scene as it was in England in Victorian days. The services for the blacks were, we gathered, more informal than those for the whites. Some of the preachers had something of the fervour of Scottish Presbyterian ministers. This story is necessarily second-hand but it illustrates a punishment which was attractively unique. The Minister, describing the horrors of the Hell that his parishioners were in danger of heading for, intoned 'And there shall be weeping and wailing and gnashing of teeth.' A voice from the congregation: 'But Parson I ain't got no teeth.' 'Den de Lord will give you Hell on de gums!'

Whether for whites or blacks, the schools in Macon, like all the other schools in the United States, had as a primary objective to bring the children up as good Americans. Teaching about American history and the Constitution of the United States was, therefore, very important. So was the teaching of English, which all immigrants were expected to learn if they did not already know it.

But in recent years a new problem has arisen. Large numbers of Hispanics, most of them Mexican, have been streaming across the southern border of the United States and many of them are not learning English. This immigration does not yet threaten the power structure of the USA and whites will continue to be preponderant within it. But even ten years ago few people, I fancy, would have forecast that in the not-too-distant future blacks and Hispanics together would outnumber whites and that already today there would be talk of a defensive Amendment to the Constitution making English the official language of the United States.

The great distances from Georgia onwards impressed us, symbolised best, perhaps, by the scale of the Grand Canyon: between four and seventeen miles wide, 5000 feet deep and in length equalling the distance from London to Brighton. We rode down into it on mules; an eight-hour trip, of which seven were spent riding a mule. On the first rather dramatic serpentine track down the face of the cliff, with a sheer drop of several hundred feet below, the guide encouraged us: 'You don't want to worry.

The mule may not care for you, but he cares for himself.'

The distances helped us too to appreciate that in some senses America is more like a continent than a country and needs to be governed accordingly. The comparison may seem ridiculous because of the difference in scale, but in principle the problem of distribution of powers between different levels in the United States was mirrored in microcosm by the same problem in education in the United Kingdom.

In each case the balance may change with the generations. In Britain after decentralisation between the wars there had been extreme concentration of power at the centre during the Second World War and it was largely due to this that Britain's resources were more efficiently mobilised than those of any other country, including Germany. It was by no means entirely due to the massive vote for Labour in 1945 that the post-war social reforms contained a strong element of influence from the centre. This applied to the National Health Service and the National Social Security Scheme which resulted from the Beveridge Report as well as, in education, the increase in the statutory powers of the Ministry. In this last case the process was carried further. It could be argued without too much exaggeration that the consensus which followed the Butler Act for twenty years relied fundamentally on the power and cohesion of three people: Dr William Alexander (later Lord Alexander) Secretary of the Association of Education Committees; Ronald (later Sir Ronald) Gould, Secretary-General of the National Union of Teachers; and the Minister of Education, advised by his Permanent Secretary.

In this narrative I have momentarily by-passed Texas, a thing that anyone does at his peril, and which I should not wish to do, if only because in Houston there was an architect who made our visit there as interesting as Larry Perkins had made our visit to Chicago.

William (Bill) Caudill, with whom I had sat on a panel at the school convention in Atlantic City, was the senior partner in the firm of Caudill, Rowlett & Scott, later to become one of the best-known firms in the United States – and not only in educational building. Youngish, sturdily built, not tall, a teddy bear of a man, with an occasional stammer slight enough to be attractive rather than embarrassing, he was, like Stirrat Johnson-Marshall, a thinker about architecture as well as a practising architect.

The professional likeness was extraordinary. Half an hour into our first meeting Bill and I found ourselves talking the same language. His belief in team-work and in the 'problem-solving approach' and the close relationship with clients made his style almost identical with that of our Ministry's development group. But of course he had access to much greater quantity and variety of materials than we had in Britain and he made excellent use of them.

Driving towards Houston for our first meeting with him we had a brief snapshot of Texas as it was depicted in films. We realised when we were about fifty miles away that we were going to be late and I hurried into a gas station to ask the attendant if I could use the telephone. I must have been moving faster than I thought. He got his question in first. Without any preliminary greeting he asked, 'Who shot who?'

Even in those days Texas was bigger and better, and there and in California, already the fastest growing state in the Union, we saw in action the full expression of competition as a national spur. Activities like zoning of buildings and anti-pollution controls ranked low in the order of priorities and the automobile was king. Indeed, we had the impression that to an American the quality of his car was more important than that of his house. The fearsome smog-ridden sprawl of Los Angeles was one result of these attitudes and so, in British eyes, was the extravagant use of physical resources, amply available though they were.

The post-war balance struck in the United States between competition and control was completely different from that struck in Britain. This set one thinking about the comparative springs of initiative on our side of the Atlantic and what, if anything, governments should do to try to redress any imbalance. I thought that in a country like Britain with limited physical resources ('an island of coal surrounded by fish' according to Mr Aneurin Bevan) the greatest single contribution that the government could make was to create the conditions in which everyone could be educated to the best advantage. The failure to achieve this objective, in spite of the high hopes of the Butler Act was due in part to the relatively low standing of the Ministry in the hierarchy of government. For a brief period in the 1950s under Sir David Eccles it looked as though attitudes might be going to change, but change on any serious scale did not materialise. It was an important opportunity missed.

Meanwhile, less serious thoughts were occupying our minds as we worked steadily northwards and mixed sightseeing in such places as San Francisco and Yosemite with a study of school building in California. The administration was well organised, the guidance from state level downwards, if a bit detailed, was intelligent and the pace of building kept up with the very fast growth of the population.

In architecture there were fewer direct lessons for Britain, for almost all the schools were single-storey and well spread out because there was plenty of land. Great attention was paid to ventilation and to protection from excessive sunlight in that hot country and in most schools there was air conditioning. Many buildings were stylish in their use of materials, but they cost more than we could have afforded and, as to expense, in many American schools the teachers were accustomed to keeping the electric lights on all day.

North from San Francisco was almost pure holiday. We found that we were following in the recent footsteps of Professor Sir Richard Livingstone, the noted historian from Oxford. As so often, the title and its appurtenances were hard to understand, especially by young American children. The small son of the family with whom we stayed in Portland, Oregon, asked him, 'Tell me, Sir Richard, did you leave your horse and armour in England?' All this time the regular correspondence between my father and Ella had been continuing. His latest contribution was remarkable for striking an unreservedly affectionate note. 'You write like Boswell about Johnson, but what is Boswell doing?'

Although at Seattle we still had 2000 miles to go by road and 3000 by sea, our thoughts turned to home and to my future at work. Owing to a retirement higher up there was going to be a vacancy at Under-Secretary level, a grade above mine, and although, at thirty-six, I was young for it, promotion at that age would not be a record and the whole school-building operation had attracted much favourable attention. But a letter from John Maud told me that it was not to be. An older man had got the promotion and the general tenor of his message was 'I have you well in mind for promotion – but not yet.' I was not to know that this disappointing piece of news was to be followed during the next six months by two experiences that were much worse.

Back then across the continent, clocking up the 20,000th mile just before we reached Cambridge, Mass., where some friends of Ella's had very kindly lent us their house for the last three weeks of my Fellowship. The owners of the house, Eric and Marne Schroeder, were on holiday at their home on the island of Naushon, off Cape Cod, which Marne's family owned.

Eric was a remarkable man, English by origin, with the intuitive unpredictability of a genius. He was an Arabist of great distinction, who was on the faculty of Harvard and was proud of the fact that only Shakespeare and he were required reading in seven departments at the university. He made an authoritative translation of the Koran and compiled a book entitled *Muhammad's People*, which traced the history of the Arab world by means of quotations from Arab literature. Eric's sister Kate was also married to an American, by an extraordinary coincidence Marne Schroeder's cousin Howell Forbes. Kate was one of Ella's oldest friends in the ballet world.

The house, in Follen Street, close to Harvard, was a three-storey timber house, rather dark in the daytime and, as some people thought, spooky. On one side there was a narrow driveway leading to the side entrance. On the first floor there was an unusual arrangement. A corridor ran straight from the front all the way to the back of the house with an archway in the middle separating two staircases, one down to the front door and the other down to the back. Our bedroom was at the back of the house, overlooking the garage, outside which our car was parked.

The night of 7 August 1951, a date that we have good reason to remember, was sultry and rather stifling. Ella went to bed without any nightdress because of the heat. For some reason it occurred to me that on previous nights I ought really to have been locking all the windows and the front and back doors before we went to bed. So I did that on 7 August, except that the lock on the back door was broken. Close on midnight (the first of two occasions in my life when midnight was associated with drama) Ella woke me and said, 'I think there's someone in the house.' I got up, with my pyjama jacket open (I remember), looked over the banisters down the back stairs in the dark, saw no-one else there, and walked towards the archway. I said 'We had better have some light on this scene,' switched on the light, walked through the archway and was faced two feet away in the corner of the stairway by a young man in jeans with a sailing knife raised ready for struggle.

It was a shock and my words came with difficulty. 'What are you doing here?' 'What are you doing here?' he asked in reply. I thought of asking what his name was but reckoned that that would get us no further. It seemed urgent to get rid of the knife, so I grabbed at his wrist, but his reaction was quicker and he stabbed me in the chest. We then tumbled together over and over down fifteen stairs rather like a Hollywood fight, though I daresay the stuntmen would have made a better job of it, and then, still with arms engaged, we got to our feet by the front door. Ella had run down the back stairs – to add to the bizarre nature of the scene, still naked – and realised from the boy's looks what the truth of the matter might be. 'You're the Schroeder boy,' she said.

It was indeed so. Mark, rising seventeen, had been sailing on his uncle's yacht up to Maine and, as it happened, Kate had given him a new sailing knife as a present. Because of favourable winds the yacht arrived in Maine earlier than expected. Mark took a train to Boston, but missed his connection to take him on to a cousin's house outside Cambridge. So, as it was nearly midnight, he decided to sleep the night at home. No one had told him that we would be there, so he thought we were intruders. No one had told us that he might come as he wasn't expected to do so.

At that point I fainted. Mark, scared that I might be dead, ran out of the house. Ella got a helpful telephone operator, who quickly summoned the police and an ambulance. When I came to, lying on the stairs, Ella was dressed and a cop burst in, took one look at me and said, 'This guy's been stabbed.' Off we went to the hospital with ambulance and police sirens screaming and lights flashing. Somehow the police collected Mark as well. He and Ella sat on opposite sides of the waiting room while I was carried straight on to an operating table. While the doctors got to work one cop stood by my head taking a statement as a precaution when the doctor told me that the knife wound was an inch from my heart.

Luckily, as so often happens, humour then entered upon the scene. A man came up to me and asked, 'What's your religion?' Not very encouraging! I replied, 'Church of England.' 'What *is* the Church of England?' he asked. My reply seemed to satisfy him. 'I'll tell you another time. I think all you want to know is that I'm not a Roman Catholic.' Five minutes later another question. The doctors were not able to get at the damage satisfactorily, so an official asked me, 'Do we have your permission to destroy your pyjama jacket?' 'Ah, a fellow administrator' I thought - and felt strangely encouraged. But after another five minutes morale sank again as the first voice repeated 'What did you say your religion was?'

By this time with, as I later discovered, a pint of blood swilling around in my chest, the pain was fairly considerable and it was not at all encouraging to hear one doctor say to the other, 'If we did that, he'd die.' This spurred my determination to recover. For three quarters of an hour Ella was waiting anxiously for news. At last she was told that all looked like being well. And so it was – except that a few days later I had to go into a nursing home to have some displaced blood drawn off my back.

Meanwhile Eric, whose interests extended to astrology, cast up horoscopes for Mark and me and seemed reassured to discover that on that particular day Mark's stars and mine were due to come into violent conflict. It was all a most unfortunate misunderstanding. If only one of a number of things had been done – or not done – the encounter would not have turned out as it did. When survival was no longer at stake, I felt sorry for Mark. It was a heavy burden for a young man to bear. It is good to report that for many years now he has been farming successfully in Vermont.

But back in 1951 the procedure was not yet complete. In such a case in the United States the file may not be closed until it has been established that neither party wishes to make a 'complaint' against the other – with money usually involved, of course. So one morning Eric, Mark and Ella and I found ourselves sitting on a bench outside a judge's chambers talking to the very nice and helpful police sergeant who was in charge of the case. A rather pompous clerk came out of the judge's room and said, 'Sergeant Frato, bring this situation in.' The situation got to its eight feet and walked in to sit on another bench.

The Judge's first remark surprised me. 'I reckon I know something about this case. I read it in the newspapers.' Then – to me – 'Do you wish to bring a complaint against this boy?' 'No,' I said. 'I'm supposed to be on a goodwill visit, so I wouldn't think it appropriate.' 'A very fine attitude,' commented the Judge, and ordered the file to be closed. The advice and help which the British Consul-General had kindly offered was not required and, fortunately for the state of my bank balance, the Commonwealth Fund footed the medical bills.

In spite of this dramatic experience, the Fellowship achieved exactly what a sabbatical year was designed to achieve. Apart from the many contacts which remained through future years, some of them to this day, the professional experience of a completely different environment was invaluable. We received a number of kind letters of farewell and au revoir. The one that pleased us most was from Dr Walter Cocking in New York. 'We love you both. You have made a host of friends all over America.'

Back in England, but not yet in the best of shape, I returned in time for the general election of 1951, in which the Tories under Winston Churchill returned to power. To an electorate chafing under continuing shortages and multifarious controls, the slogan 'Set the people free!' pointed to an attractive future. But even with the help of Marshall Aid the economic prospect at home was not very exciting. Abroad the now ageing Prime Minister presided over the slow dissolution of the Empire he loved and felt uncomfortable, as many Britons did, with the growing manifestations of the power and ambitions of some of the emerging nations.

Many people took a more positive view than did the Prime Minister about the Empire, seeing its gradual transmutation into a Commonwealth of independent nations as a constructive move, none the less enlightened because it was, in sober truth, the only practical course to take. But few yet had a vision of an EEC, still less of Britain becoming a member of it. We still cherished the famous headline 'Fog in the Channel. Continent isolated.'

After the general election we waited anxiously – as civil servants always do – to hear who our new Minister was to be. Usually the Permanent Secretary hears first: sometimes the Minister's Private Secretary. On this occasion the information came from an unexpected source. Two workmen arrived. 'Who are you?' 'We're from the Ministry of Works. We've come to convert a lavatory for a lady.' Our new Minister was to be Florence Horsburgh. To be the only senior woman in a government led by Mr Churchill was a less than ideal assignment and as Education was set more or less on a 'steady as you go' course there was nothing particularly exciting for her to do. But she was a very nice person, who had acquired much merit as an assiduous party worker and I think she found her officials, from John Maud downwards, helpful.

As for myself, the extremely able David Nenk had kept the administrative side of A and B Branch going healthily forward. His brain had a very sharp cutting edge – and so did his tongue. There were those who thought him the most brilliant civil servant of his generation – certainly of the Ministry of Education.

At this stage, there were thought among the Ministry's bookmakers to be four candidates for Permanent Secretary of the Ministry in ten or twelve years' time. In alphabetical order the first was Neville Heaton, the most introspective, but also the most senior, who had done an outstanding job during the war in working closely with Sir Maurice Holmes on the Butler Act. The second David Nenk. The third myself. The fourth Toby (later Sir Toby) Weaver, who probably knew more about the process of education than the rest of us and whose intellect was sharp and clear. In 1951 you could probably have got odds of 100 to 1 if you had declared that, as in fact happened, none of us would ever become Permanent Secretary of the Ministry. In David Nenk's case he sadly died of cancer in 1960 at the early age of forty-four.

For me, to be back in A and B Branch was rather like feeling 'hung over' after a year-long party in the United States, marvellous in spite of its dénouement. There then occurred a most unwelcome development. Mr Ernest Marples, Chairman of the Cabinet's Building Committee on Economy in the use of Materials, seconded by Mr Hugh (now Lord) Molson, proposed a speedy independent enquiry into the school building operation on the grounds that it was uneconomical in cost, materials and labour. Mr Harry (later Lord) Pilkington was appointed by the Minister to conduct it as a one-man investigation.

Shortly after this had been announced I was discovered to have contracted tuberculosis of the lungs, so that removed me from the scene for what was clearly going to be at least six months and quite possibly a year. The fact that it was established that I must have caught it in the United States was no consolation. So, apart from this major problem about my health, I was unable to be on the scene during the Pilkington enquiry. I wrote to him, with a rather anxious confidence, that perhaps it was no bad way to test the efficiency of an organisation by removing the head of it during the enquiry. A few weeks later, as I lay in bed at home awaiting admission to a sanatorium, a letter arrived from Harry Pilkington. 'I didn't want to write until I was absolutely certain of the tenor of my Report. I have now completed the first rough draft. It goes further than being a mere acquittal: it says that the work that your branch has done is so good and well-conceived that other departments might try to see what they can learn from it.'

The report has been described as a paean of praise, commending particularly the inter-disciplinary approach. It had been my first chance to create a 'team of mixed skills' which had so impressed me at the Ministry of Supply and was to form a favourite theme in later years. The credit was shared by all the partners in the enterprise. Naturally it did wonders for my morale. Several months in a sanatorium in Surrey did not. Some patients were in a small ward, but most of us were in individual cubicles with most of one side consisting of large windows that were always kept fully open. When it rained the nurses put a mackintosh sheet over the bed.

My physical strength was negligible, although drugs existed by then that more or less guaranteed me against death. The mental impact was severe. I had not the endurance to listen to the radio for any length of time and for reading my span of attention just about sufficed for an article in *Reader's Digest*. On the wall at the foot of the bed was a single picture, changed once a month by a lady from the Red Cross, with whom it was nice to have a chat. Luckily the nurses seconded from St. Thomas's were delightful and I remain affectionate friends to this day.

I was much luckier than some of my fellow patients. They had been in the sanatorium for one, two, or in one case three years. They had what I came to call 'the courage of the long haul', harder than courage in the quick moment of danger. Many years later this knowledge was professionally valuable to me. A Permanent Secretary holds a lot of people's secrets. It was therefore very useful to understand that some of my colleagues did need the courage of the long haul in their careers and their domestic problems, which impinged on their careers.

The doctors refused to give me any information, in particular about when I might be allowed to get up, a critical point in my recovery. 'You must learn, Mr Part, to take yourself out of gear.'

Solitary confinement was not my scene, but visitors were allowed only once a week, except for a very special reason. 'The trouble with you,' said the superintendent, refusing permission on one occasion, 'is that you have too many friends.'

Shortly after that the skies seemed to brighten momentarily when an attractive young woman stood in the doorway. 'May I come in?' she said. 'Of course. Who are you?' 'I'm a bed occupational therapist.' Various unrealistically ambitious thoughts flashed across my mind, but she quickly made it clear that the bed was for me and not for her and that the idea was for me to choose between tapestry and knitting! One day the sister asked me whether I could play chess as there was a Yugoslav patient who would like a game. 'Just about,' I said. It quickly became apparent that he was much better at it than me. After two games the sister came to tell me that I must stop playing chess. 'The difficulty is,' she said, 'that you are trying to win.' I began to think that training in Buddhism would be an advantage.

After six months I was allowed to get up and after seven I was released early 'because you have a good home,' said the superintendent. Ella and I went to an hotel in Torquay where we picked up an interesting piece of worldly wisdom from a waiter. It was in the days when most people took breakfast in the dining room. 'You can always tell whether they're married,' he confided to us. 'If they're not she says: "Darling, will you have some sugar in your tea?"' After Torquay a short visit to St Moritz, generously financed by my father, and chats with a most agreeable hotel doctor, who told us what advice he gave to women patients who had 'fallen in love' with their ski instructor. He was clearly headed for retirement as a rich man!

I returned to work in the spring of 1953 to find Britain, as I thought, approaching a watershed. We had survived the war, endured the prolonged post-war shortages, started on three major social reforms and begun to adjust, reluctantly, to our new diminished standing in the world. Our prestige and pride were less diminished than our standing, the pride being illustrated best, perhaps, by the coincidence of the young Queen's coronation and the announcement of the British conquest of Everest.

The welfare state was developing fast and the Civil Service could not claim that the officials at the Treasury (or anywhere else) were pressing Ministers to tackle Britain's increasing lack of international competitiveness in the economic sphere. The political urge to do so was not great either. Britain still had a healthy share of world trade and established between the mid 1950s and 1970 the fastest rate of growth in its economic history, faster, indeed, than that during those fifteen years of any of our future partners in the EEC. We had 'full employment' and an increasing proportion of the population were able to buy such things as television sets and motor cars. All this leading to Harold Macmillan's factually accurate, if economically misleading, claim in 1937 that 'You have never had it so good.' The fact that he never used quite those words is not, perhaps, important. They certainly represented the tenor of his message.

Socially and economically Britain remained a paternalistic structure. Cracks began to appear in the mid 1950s when rock'nroll burst upon us in 'Rock around the clock', girls stopped dressing like their mothers, and one of the first priorities of young people was to make themselves mobile on motor-bikes and, before long, in motor cars. All this was seen as a revolt, a statement of independence, or a move towards it. Few saw developments at that time as the start of a movement away from a paternalistic society towards something more American, a society in which the initiative would, and should, lie more with the consumer, 'consumer' meaning not just a customer of the retail trade. The balance of influence was starting to move towards the people as a whole, so that those in government, whether politicians or civil servants, would need not only to be more aware of developments outside Whitehall, but to take them into full account in their assessments.

Such a change of balance is a hard lesson for central government, because it points on the one hand to a diminution of their power and, on the other, to the need for greater skills in the construction of policies. There would be more (and more various) prime movers, whether individuals or organisations, those civil servants who helped to make policies would need to get cleverer at scene-setting and those many who provided services would need to become more sensitive to the requirements of the public.

Lest it be thought that to propound this argument is to lean too heavily towards a Tory approach, it is not intended to do so. These developments were underlying shifts in the nature of the body politic and any government would have to find its own solution to the handling of them. One of the first to appreciate the nature of these changes was Sir David Eccles, who followed Florence Horsburgh as Minister of Education in 1954. He was – and is – highly intelligent and sensitive to social changes. His political thinking and his interest in economic matters (which ultimately got him into trouble with his colleagues) belied the apparent air of superiority which was reinforced by his meticulously tailored appearance. He was the only politician of whom it was said that his chances of rising further would have been enhanced if he had gone to a less good tailor!

By this time Gilbert Flemming had at last come into his inheritance as Permanent Secretary. Mr Churchill had insisted on John Maud being moved sideways to Fuel and Power after he had overstepped the mark by issuing to LEAs a politically sensitive circular that aroused criticism without getting Miss Horsburgh's approval.

I had returned to work in 1953 and got my promotion to Under-Secretary as Head of Schools Branch the following year. Then at the beginning of 1956 there came an unexpected development with exciting potential, which brought me into close touch with David Eccles and his ideas. It was to prove a congenial alliance and a good illustration of the respective tasks of Ministers and civil servants with Gilbert Flemming as, so to speak, moderator.

David's ideas about education policy were well developed. 'Never under-rate the importance of education,' he used to say. The gist of his thinking was that, as the years went by, people should, and would, become better educated – or at least better informed. He cited the importance of television, increased by the fairly recent start-up of independent television. People's demands for more information would grow into greater demands for participation. Greater pressure for increasing decentralisation would follow automatically. The quality of education at that time was inadequate and there was one big missing dimension – the development of technical education. The government as a whole were beginning to have a sense of this gap, and it was increased by the prospect of the launching of the Russian Sputnik into space. People were impressed too by the German post-war recovery, assisted by its known quality of technical education and its important contribution to what became known as the 'German economic miracle' under Adenauer.

It was decided that I should transfer from Schools Branch to 'Further Education' Branch, which covered technical, commercial, agricultural, art and architectural education with adult education added in. This was completely strange territory to me

– and, deplorably, to most of the Ministry's administrators: a highly specialised world full of initials such as HND and ONC and the titles of various craft qualifications supervised by the City and Guilds of London Institute. It had quite close links with management and unions and relationships which varied from the cordial to the caustic with the professional bodies such as the various Institutions in the engineering world.

By contrast with the schools, the technical colleges had the role of entrepreneurs. They responded to demand – often demand which they themselves had created. At the higher end they had ambitions for university status, coupled with an inferiority complex in relation to the universities, which the universities were careful to cultivate. Incidentally, this attitude extended to the Ministry itself and somewhere around 1960 I was severely taken to task at a discussion dinner of some size at the Athenaeum by forecasting that one day before long the universities would come under the aegis of the Ministry instead of the Treasury.

Further Education was a stimulating challenge. As an administrative task it had much in common with my earlier work on school building – at the behest of Ministers (though this time with much wider Ministerial support) to expand and upgrade a politically sensitive operation. The 'team of mixed skills' came to the fore again, though not in a formal organisational sense, but the Under-Secretary and the Chief Inspector, Bill Shelley, worked in close partnership. Like school building, it involved a lot of travel and personal contact. Like school building too, it required a fair amount of evangelism. Indeed, at a meeting of a Cabinet committee of senior officials in the late 1950s the chairman from the Treasury addressed me as 'Young Lochinvar'. Again, like school building, there were tensions – sometimes extreme tensions – between some of the partners in the enterprise.

On succeeding Freddy Bray, a technical education HMI turned administrator, my first task was to draft a White Paper announcing the government's policies. This exercise provided an interesting illustration of the interplay between a Minister and his officials. Before my appointment the senior officials had secured approval to the capital expenditure over an unstated period of £70 million for technical college building – a lot of money in those days and an essential prelude to significant progress. David Eccles' energetic and skilful advocacy and the support of the Prime Minister, Anthony Eden, resulted in the endorsement of this figure.

Then came the drafting of a White Paper announcing the general shape of the government's attitude. It was later described as 'a tract for the times' on the one hand by those who agreed with its sentiments and on the other by those who thought it contained too few practical proposals. For David Eccles in particular it was an important document, the start of a major new initiative closely affecting the government's reputation and his own. He himself drafted an introduction central to the setting of the scene and, as was the custom, he sent it to me for comment. It didn't seem to me to highlight quite the right points and I submitted an alternative version. As the matter was urgent, he summoned me down to his elegant country house in Hampshire the following Saturday to discuss the matter.

The Permanent Secretary who, in line with Whitehall procedure had a copy of each version, decided against intervening, but I expect that he and the Minister had a talk about it.

Sitting in his study the Minister politely made it clear, as he was entitled to do, that he wanted his own version or something very like it. We discussed a few amendments and settled the draft. Afterwards he gave me lunch with his charming wife, Sybil, and his older son John, and then went off shooting while Sybil drove me to the railway station. It was then my task to draft the rest of the White Paper for submission to him and the Cabinet.

After its publication it was for us in Further Education Branch to put flesh on the bones of the policy. At the craft level this was fairly easy as the set-up was well established in consultation with industrial management and the trade unions. We were still, however, far from the days when the unions could be brought to agree with the practice in the armed forces that the length of an apprenticeship should be measured by the standard reached without reference to the time served. Quite a few employers dragged their feet on this issue too as the longer-serving apprentices represented useful cheap labour. For technicians the lines of a policy were straightforward, for the National Certificates (part-time) were well established and so, to a lesser degree, were the full-time Diplomas. The main shortcoming was that there were not enough people training to be technicians and too few technicians were employed by industry. It was rather like trying to run an army with a shortage of warrant officers and senior NCOs.

The argument – and it was violent – came at professional level. It could have been billed as the technical colleges versus the LEAs versus two schools of thought in the Ministry versus the professional institutions versus the universities. It went to the root of the structure and role of the leading technical colleges. There was also the question of the pattern of technical colleges as a whole. Being the kind of places that they were, they had 'grown like Topsy'. Was this a healthy market-related trend which should be allowed to continue or was it not cost effective, particularly as regards staff and equipment?

The undergraduate degree-level work (there was practically no post-graduate work) depended on external validation by London University and therefore left little room for innovation by the colleges. A system had developed of giving seventy five per cent grant for advanced work (post-GCE 'A' level or the equivalent) to selected colleges. By 1956 there were about two dozen of these. None restricted themselves to advanced work only. The contrast between these colleges and the great *Technische Hochschulen* on the continent, still more with the Massachusetts Institute of Technology in the United States, was stark. In any event some of the universities considered that they (or parts of them) fulfilled that role, though none of them in those days had the same close links with industry as those abroad did.

The first British reform, which preceded the White Paper by some months, was uncontroversial. The Ministry established a National Council for Technological Awards. The choice, as Chairman, of Lord Hives, the Chairman of Rolls-Royce, was fortunate as, apart from his own merits, he clearly represented excellence. The council members were drawn from universities, industry, the technical professional organisations and the technical colleges. With a view largely to replacing the external degree of London University so far as technical colleges were concerned, the council set as its first award the

Diploma in Technology. (The use of the title 'degree' was limited in those days by statute to universities at first degree level.) The colleges would design the courses and they would be approved by the NCTA and monitored by them.

The chief bone of contention was the structure of the technical colleges. On this subject the officials at the Ministry and those at the professional institutions, led by the Institution of Electrical Engineers, were literally not on speaking terms. The institutions wanted a very small number of colleges at the top of the structure concentrating entirely on degree level work. This was mainly in order to make the best use of a necessarily limited number of able teachers. The Ministry officials and most of the senior technical HMIs were not prepared to contemplate such a radical change from the traditions they had grown up with. What, they asked, would happen to such places as the Regent Street Polytechnic and the Brighton College of Technology, both of them highly respected in the technical education world?

This was an awkward situation for a newcomer to walk into, especially in view of the close partnership that he would need to establish with the Chief Inspector for Technical Education. But after listening to the professional institutions on the one hand and the Ministry and its HMIs on the other I became convinced – especially on account of the cost-effectiveness and on the point about teachers – that the institutions were right. I then came to think that the same two arguments pointed to a rationalisation of the structure of the colleges as a whole. The Minister approved this approach.

The outcome was a clearly-defined structure. At the top a small number (probably ten in the end) of Colleges of Advanced Technology at university level was proposed. We hesitated for a moment about the likely public impact of the initials CAT, but came to the conclusion that if things went well 'the CATs' would come to be regarded with affection as well as esteem. Luckily this turned out to be so.

Below the CATs would be about two dozen regional colleges with quite a bit of advanced full-time, as well as part-time, work. This was the category to which Regent Street and Brighton had to belong as they both declined to jettison their non-advanced work.

In diplomatic terms this was a pity because the principals of those two colleges were among the most able and influential of all the technical college leaders. But if we had made an exception in their favour the credibility of an important element in the new structure would have been jeopardised. The next tier would be 175 area colleges with only part-time advanced work and, finally, local colleges with no advanced work at all.

Much persuasion was required. For this the National Advisory Council on Education for Industry and Commerce was actively used for two-way communication. It was a large body consisting of representatives of the colleges, the LEAs, the universities and teachers' organisations. It was headed by Lt Gen Sir Ronald Weeks, then the chairman of Vickers. We bounced ideas as well as proposals off them and they did not hesitate to express views of their own. The great thing was to keep up a fast enough momentum of successive proposals so that everyone had a sense of being a partner in a campaign to develop technical education. Two or three years later (by this time with my old friend Harry Pilkington in the chair) the Ministry developed a procedure for submitting to the council every six months a report on what had been done during the last half year and our proposals for action in the following six months. (This was a technique which I later took with me to the Department of Trade and Industry for internal use.)

As the years went by we covered such matters as a post-graduate award by the CATs (though the primary responsibility for this lay with the NCAA), commercial education (which included the invention of the National Diplomas in Business Studies), agricultural and architectural education, new developments in training for the hotel and catering trade and, of course, the annual building programmes for technical education.

Art was dealt with by a separate National Advisory Council full of prima donnas. It was set up in 1959. Its first main achievement, in partnership with the National Council for Diplomas in Art and Design under Sir John Summerson (established in 1961) was to initiate the now familiar diploma in Art and Design (Dip. A.D.). The courses leading to this diploma were to be conceived as a liberal education in art at university level. Specialisation should be related not to individual subjects but to a broad area such as fine art, graphic design, three dimensional design and textiles and fashion.

Victor Pasmore, the well-known painter, wanted to know why on earth anyone needed any passes at GCE Ordinary Level to qualify for one of these courses at the age of eighteen. 'I,' he said, 'never was able to pass the School Certificate.' The chairman, Sir William Coldstream, himself a distinguished painter, explained that for most people fine art accounted for only a small proportion of any course. Most of the students would be going into careers in graphic, fashion or industrial design.

It was not all growth and expansion. At one stage we (that is, the Ministry) had to cut the number of art courses quite severely and to close one whole school, at Willesden. The students were, understandably, indignant and decided to protest by carrying a coffin into the Ministry. They unloaded it from the truck and carried it in the approved fashion on their shoulders. As they came into the building at Curzon Street House the Parliamentary Secretary, Dennis Vosper, a polite man if ever there was one, came out of the lift. He put on his hat and then, seeing the coffin, did the only thing a gentleman could do, which was to take his hat off again. He told me later that it was not until he got out into the street that he realised his mistake.

Public relations were easier (or perhaps one should say less difficult) for the Ministry of Education than for most other departments. Education was, maybe unfortunately, not of great interest to the mass media in those days. The controversies were frequent but specialised – like relations with the churches, the row about the CATs and the size of the school building programme. One of the few subjects that interested the national press was negotiations about teachers' pay – and then mainly because of the relationship between the settlement for teachers and those for other professional people. There were no juicy issues like race relations in the schools, arguments about sex education or whether competition is disreputable. In the 1950s educational issues were not going to produce a positive answer to the perennial editorial question 'Will this item sell more newspapers?' A notable exception was *The Economist*, which employed three very intelligent women educational correspondents in succession.

Relations with the educational and, when necessary, with the relevant specialist publications such as the *Architects' Journal* were, however, very important. Publications such as *The Times Educational Supplement* and *Education* (the journal of the Association of Education Committees) were well-informed, influential in the educational world and, on the whole, accurate. Ministers were, of course, active in this sphere and we had a small but good press office. But informal relations between senior officials and the press could be very helpful. It was worth spending quite a bit of time to establish and maintain mutual confidence. In one other respect Education had a less difficult task than many other departments: the number of its constituents was smaller, so it was easier to cover the waterfront.

All this was some years before television began to 'feel its oats' and was able, in effect, to summon Ministers before the cameras. In those days civil servants, naturally and correctly, avoided like the plague appearances on television and any personal exposure to publicity in the national press came mainly as a result of appearances before a select committee of Parliament. This was before the proceedings of these committees attracted much attention from the press and before some of the proceedings were recorded for radio.

When David Eccles returned to the Ministry after a spell as President of the Board of Trade he was pleased with the progress made by the operation he had initiated. 'In the short space of four years,' he said in a speech at Liverpool, 'the number of students in full-time courses has doubled and now totals 112,000. Students attending sandwich courses have increased sevenfold (from 1,400 to 10,000). The total of part-time students has grown from 400,000 to 500,000 and the number of full-time teachers has risen from 10,000 to 17,000. Finally we have authorised £100 million of new building, of which nearly half has been completed.'

So far so good. But we had started from a relatively low base, even though that base itself was considerably higher than that of the 1930s. It was worrying that only one out of every eight young people aged between sixteen and eighteen was still engaged in full-time education and that, whatever the theory, the system as a whole was not providing an adequate way forward for anything like all school leavers. A committee, chaired by Sir Geoffrey Crowther, then editor of *The Economist*, under the aegis of the Central Advisory Council for Education in England had reported in the same sense in 1959. Their report '15/18' proposed as a national objective that the proportion of pupils staying on full-time should be raised by 1979 to one in every two.

In 1959, still under Sir David Eccles, the Ministry published a White Paper entitled 'Better Opportunities in Technical Education'. It set out detailed proposals to broaden education and provide continuity between school and college, to adapt the system better to the needs of industry, to increase the variety of courses and to reduce wastage. This White Paper gave special satisfaction to those of us who felt that in all the post-war stresses and strains and with all the natural emphasis on high standards and opportunities for the most able, the needs of the rest (if anything over half of each age group) had not been adequately emphasised or catered for.

In part this was because the experts could not agree on what kind of secondary education was appropriate for this very considerable group. As a reaction from the past there was a bias against the setting of standards and a number of HMIs were strongly opposed to pupils in secondary modern schools (or those of equivalent standard in comprehensive schools) taking the School Certificate or its successor the GCE Ordinary Level, thus blocking for many pupils a way forward that should have been open to them. If 50% of the sixteen to eighteen age group were going to remain in full-time education some kind of test (or tests) at the age of 15 or 16 should have been regarded as essential. In my view the lack of urgency in implementing this White Paper contributed in an indirect but significant way to the failure to raise the capability of our boys and girls to a level adequate for our economic needs in an increasingly competitive world.

In 1960, as a new Deputy Secretary (now covering teacher training as well as further education) I was not allowed to be idle. There was experience on three committees. The first was on apprenticeship with Robert Carr MP (now Lord Carr) in the chair. But no striking progress was possible as the trade unions thought that it was not in their interests to budge from insistence on time-serving rather than standards achieved.

The second committee provided, as I think it was intended to do, a wider horizon. It was on the management of government research and development with particular reference to defence. The chairman, Sir Claud Gibb, unfortunately died soon after his appointment and Sir Solly (now Lord) Zuckerman, already a member, took over the chair. He was supported by Sir Arthur Penney (later Lord Penney), chairman of the Atomic Energy Authority, Sir Patrick Linstead (Rector of Imperial College), Sir George Edwards (chairman of the British Aircraft Corporation) and myself. We produced a less brilliant report than Lord Rothschild did a dozen years later with his invention of the concept of a 'customer/contractor' relationship between the instigators of the Requirement and the R & D operators. But we mapped out a sequence of events (in the defence field, from the operational requirement onwards) designed to produce more organised and purposeful R & D and a more effective (or perhaps one should say less ineffective) control of costs.

It was immensely stimulating to be associated with these considerable men (this is one of the pleasures of working in the Civil Service) and a relaxed relationship was established. As is so often done nowadays, we met for a final weekend in the country to complete our report. It was at Latymer, Buckinghamshire, in what was then the National Defence College. After dinner the commandant set us to play the then popular three-dimensional noughts and crosses. I suddenly realised that my three companions playing this game were all Fellows of the Royal Society. One seemed to be guided by higher mathematics, the second had a successfully forthright approach and the third treated the game as though it were a problem in structural design. In such a constellation whoever played with me as his partner was bound to lose. And so it was. But we had a lot of fun in the process.

The third committee assignment was altogether a more wide-ranging affair. The government set up a Committee on Higher Education (*all* higher education) with Lord Robbins in the chair.

The members of the committee were all powerful and experienced in their various fields – schools, universities, technical colleges, the local authorities and the world of business. Sir Keith Murray (later Lord Murray of Newhaven), chairman of the University Grants Committee, was the assessor from the universities. I was the other assessor, representing the Whitehall interests – in particular the Ministry of Education.

Lord Robbins, already distinguished as an economist, was a liberal thinker – almost a philosopher – of high intelligence, who loved playing with concepts and patterns. But he had his feet well on the ground. He was also meticulously patient with witnesses and with the Ministry of Education assessor. But explorer of ideas though he was, he was determined that the work of the committee should be solidly grounded in extensive statistical analysis. (When the report was published several volumes of statistics were attached.) This brought into prominence for the first time the then young Claus Moser (now Sir Claus), who was a junior member of the staff at the LSE, where Lionel Robbins was already an internationally famous figure.

Come Christmas 1962 the committee were moving steadily towards their conclusions. They produced an impressively comprehensive report with 178 recommendations. In spite of its scope and length Ministers were quickly convinced of its merits and the committee had the unusual distinction of hearing the Prime Minister's approval announced on the day that the report was published. It is remembered chiefly because the committee recommended that, compared with the 216,000 students in full-time higher education in Great Britain in 1962–3, places should be available for about 390,000 in 1973–4 and about 550,000 in 1980–1. The numbers actually attending were 481,000 in 1973–4 and 520,000 in 1980–1, an extremely creditable achievement.

Among other things the committee recommended that the CATs (which were by then on a direct grant basis from the Ministry) should become universities. This was indeed a necessary step in a British context if the CATs were to attract staff and students of sufficient quality. The risk was that their new status would impel them too far away from their technological emphasis and their industrial links – and in some cases this occurred. Later on the ex-CATs got caught in a severe economy drive on the universities, some of them at a critical point in their development. But in spite of these handicaps they have emerged as useful additions to the university scene.

The old problem remained of the technological inadequacy of British universities compared with the great higher technological institutions in the USA and Germany. The Robbins Committee recommended the creation of five Special Institutions for Scientific and Technological Education and Research (SISTERs), each containing 3500–4500 students, of whom half should be post-graduate students. Three of these Institutions should be developed from Imperial College and the Colleges of Science and Technology at Manchester and Glasgow. A fourth should be one of the former CATs and a fifth should be completely new. It was a great pity that this important recommendation foundered on the rock of resistance from those universities which feared to lose staff, money and prestige if they were not among the chosen few. Not until many years later did the working links between the leading universities and industry become seriously stronger.

At this stage I had the firm prospect of becoming a Permanent Secretary – 'a consummation devoutly to be wished'. Before David Eccles left the Ministry in the summer of 1962 as one of the victims of Mr Macmillan's Night of the Long Knives, he had told me on several occasions (one of them after a talk with the Prime Minister) that I would be succeeding Dame Mary Smieton as Permanent Secretary when she retired in the spring of 1963. So that news added to the joys of Christmas.

On the day after the Christmas holidays, Dame Mary said that she would like to come along and see me. I naturally said that I would come to her. But no, she preferred it the other way. Experience has taught me that when your boss arranges to come to see you (except for an informal chat) it nearly always means bad news! On this occasion it was very bad news indeed, and it emerged during our conversation that she had deliberately waited 'as I didn't want to spoil your Christmas holiday'.

She told me that the plan was for me to leave the Ministry of Education and to go on a level transfer as a Deputy Secretary to the Ministry of Works. If all went well I would succeed my friend Sir Edward Muir as Permanent Secretary when he retired in 1965. She seemed to know nothing about David Eccles' talks to me and she was not able to tell me who would succeed her. (It turned out to be Sir Herbert Andrew, aged fifty three, a Second Secretary from the Board of Trade, who, with one or two others, had been strongly recommended for promotion by Mr Edward Heath following the negotiations for Britain's entry into the EEC, which was vetoed in the end by General de Gaulle.)

Dame Mary's news was a double blow. First, it removed any prospect (forever, as it seemed to me) of finishing my Civil Service career in the department that meant so much to me. Second, to be sent to the Ministry of Works, of whose approach to architecture and building I had been critical for fifteen years, seemed an immensely unattractive alternative, even with the likelihood of becoming the Permanent Secretary a couple of years later. I asked Dame Mary for interviews with the Minister (Sir Edward Boyle) and the Head of the Civil Service (Sir Laurence Helsby) and also for a fortnight in which to make up my mind, as I would like to get advice from some of my friends in industry about the possibility of my getting a job outside the Civil Service. She said that she would certainly arrange for the first and would try to arrange for the second. When Dame Mary left my room I went out for a long and miserable walk in a Green Park covered with snow.

Sir Edward Boyle said that he must have 'someone who carries weight with the Treasury'. Sir Laurence Helsby would not give any reasons for the decision, but said that it was irreversible and that there was no alternative to the Ministry of Works. He pointed out that the Ministry was about to be spectacularly enlarged by the addition of the large Works Departments from each of the three armed services, that it would be my job to organise the merger and that the newly-named Ministry of Public Building and Works would be a worldwide organisation with a staff of over 80,000.

Of my three friends in industry, two, Sir Harold Roxbee Cox (now Lord Kings Norton), then chairman of Metal Box, and Sir George Edwards, then chairman of the British Aircraft Corporation, advised me to stay in the Civil Service at that stage, and Sir Harry Pilkington said that 'just, but only just' he shared that view, unless a particularly attractive and fortunately-timed offer were to crop up. So when, after a fortnight, Edward Muir invited me to lunch at the Athenaeum (two courses – oysters and Stilton cheese, I remember) to ask how my thoughts were moving, we had what the communiqués call a 'full and frank discussion' and I said that I intended to accept Laurence Helsby's proposal. If there had to be a move it would at least be a pleasure to work for Edward.

Perhaps it was all to the good that the first quarter of 1963 proved to be a particularly busy time. In addition to the normal work at Education, which I did not leave until March, there was extra work to finish for the Robbins Report (on higher education) because the secretary of the committee had a breakdown and his assistant had, tragically, died. At the same time I was asked to sit in on a transitional working party at the Ministry of Works to try to see that there would not be a monumental foul-up on 1st March, the date of the merger.

Finally, Sir Edward Boyle asked me to write a 'Last Will and Testament' about educational policy before I left the department. This I was very reluctant to do: he had, after all, been significantly responsible for my being denied the chance to put my ideas into practice, and perhaps unreasonably my temper was not improved by his insistence on arranging, as something of a sop, a large lunch party at Claridge's in my honour. However, I did not wish to seem too bloody-minded and wrote the 'Last Will and Testament' as requested. It included the sentence 'We call teaching a profession but we do not treat the teachers as members of a profession.' Nor were they encouraged to work towards the standing of a profession. Admittedly it would have been a long haul but had they succeeded – or even made substantial progress towards that goal, the standing and attitudes of the teachers would over time have been constructively transformed.

This opportunity missed was matched later on by the destructive attitude of Mrs Thatcher's government towards the Local Education Authorities. Impatience at the inefficiency of a few authorities, particularly in and around London, was allowed to escalate into an undeserved denigration of local authorities as a whole. Indeed there were civil servants in the Treasury who thought that local government as a whole should be replaced by a few regional authorities. This view ran counter to the tendency towards the devolution of power and influence which had first become apparent in the mid-1950s. It also risked depriving the country of the carefully constructed 'building blocks' of influence that are essential to a healthy democracy.

There was one general matter to reflect on: how should the Civil Service plan and arrange the succession to senior posts and transfer between departments? As to this, a prime task of a Permanent Secretary is to satisfy himself – and his Minister – that he has the right mix of skills at the right levels. No less important is for him to find the best way of creating the atmosphere and attitudes that he thinks right.

In 1939 the newly-formed Ministry of Supply clearly required a major infusion of businessmen, if only to organise and run the raw materials controls. In 1949 the traditional Civil Service could not produce talents appropriate to man the Architects and Building Branch of the Ministry of Education – and in particular its development group. But for most departments the conventional mix of staff was thought to be adequate. The professionals, especially the scientists and technologists, did not get enough of a look-in, partly because the Civil Service did not attract able enough professionals (except for some economists) to compete on level terms *as administrators* with the recently much-abused arts graduates and partly because top management did not go out of its way to arrange special training and learning experience for them.

When the first Department of Trade and Industry was formed in 1970 we thought it desirable to appoint as temporary civil servants some forty businessmen to fill senior posts in the department. Occasionally the arrival of a single man would be particularly influential. Following a report to the Civil Service Department by a businessman and a Second Permanent Secretary about accountants (or lack of them) in the Civil Service a Head of the Government Accountancy Service was imported from the private sector and placed in the Department of Trade and Industry because that was where the most challenging commercial work needed to be done. The post has since been transferred, rightly or wrongly, to the Treasury.

A more spectacular impact was made by the appointment by Mr Heath as Prime Minister of Lord Rothschild as Head of the Central Policy Review Staff (familiarly known as the Think Tank). This group was intended to help keep the government on a steady strategic course and to challenge the establishment on any special issues which might be referred to it. Lord Rothschild's extremely original mind, his very high intelligence and his mathematical capability combined with commercial experience to make him the perfect – and perhaps unrepeatable – choice. Indeed, most Prime Ministers do not want to repeat the experiment. They feel the need to have closely alongside a fairly small group of able people, including a suitable mix of old and young, with a view to making sure that the central drive of the government is coherent and sustained.

Departmental Ministers often want to feel themselves reinforced by some advisers guaranteed to share their political inclinations. Constitutionally Ministers are supposed to rely on their Junior Ministers for this, but most of them fail to make adequate use of these people and, in any event, some of the work needed is more expert and detailed than the average Junior Minister can be expected to handle. Moreover, however adequately the Civil Service addresses itself, as it should, to the task of helping the government along the road that it has been elected to travel two or three politically sympathetic expert advisers can sometimes play a useful part.

As for the Service itself, the arrangements for planning the careers of promising staff and promoting them when they reached the topmost posts have gradually become more organised inter-departmentally. By contrast with earlier years it would now be very unusual for anyone to become a Permanent Secretary (or come to that a Deputy Secretary) without having served in more than one department, and the general policy (though it didn't happen to apply in my case) is that this experience should include a spell in the Treasury or the Cabinet Office so as to give the person some experience of seeing life from the centre. This is a good idea, even though all wisdom does not reside at the centre – as some people think it does!

The decision on appointing a Permanent Secretary is taken by the Prime Minister on the recommendation of the Head of the Civil Service, who will have consulted the departmental Minister concerned and a small standing committee of senior Permanent Secretaries. It is beyond human nature to be completely objective, but great efforts are made by the officials concerned to get as near objectivity as possible. There are the obvious qualifications: intellectual capability, relevant track record, experience of Parliament and the outside world (often nowadays including countries abroad), understanding of finance and, above all, good relations with Ministers and the ability and inclination to manage – and to manage efficiently – the almost invariably large and dispersed organisation of which he is in charge.

But there are other more intangible qualities to look for. I said of Edward Muir on his retirement

> He is a man of authority, a man of considerate fairness and a man of honour. You can only be this kind of person if you have courage and compassion. He has needed both of them, sometimes – alas – in full measure. He also has that great quality of judgement which in a senior civil servant is the indispensable ally of intellect and experience and he holds to that most useful article of faith which declares that neither logic nor policies must be allowed to stand in the way of common sense.

It was Edward who had on his desk a quotation from Benjamin Franklin, from which he drew strength:-

> We must not in the Course of Publick Life expect *immediate* Approbation and *immediate* grateful Acknowledgement of our Services. – But let us persevere thro' Abuse and even Injury. The internal Satisfaction of a good Conscience is always present, and Time will do us Justice in the Minds of the People, even of those at present the most prejudic'd against us.

What the Civil Service has to offer is its continuing experience of the art and science of government. It is not the civil servant's job to be a political partisan. If it were his position would become untenable on a change of government. But he must take on in some degree the coloration of the party in power so that he may fulfil his task of helping the government to move in the direction in which it was elected to move.

Ministers sometimes say that the Civil Service is resistant to change. (In Mrs Shirley Williams' phrase 'a superb braking mechanism.') And sometimes this must seem to be true because civil servants have considerable practical experience of government and it is their job to point out what they think will work and what won't. Anyone who knows anything about the way in which an election manifesto is compiled would not claim that all the ideas cooked up by candlelight will flourish in the light of day.

The fear of making a mistake or a misjudgement, which tends to be held against a civil servant for too long, may make the middle ranks too cautious, but the high-fliers are almost by definition specially adept at change – making at the behest of Ministers or of their own volition. Senior civil servants, after all, live with change: it is the bread-and-butter of their existence. But this is not the same thing as saying that a senior civil servant should jump to attention whenever a Minister – or even a Prime Minister – speaks, salute and say 'Yes, Minister' or 'Yes, Prime Minister: it shall be done immediately.' Discussion and argument are part of the process of good government, but civil servants are trained to remember that the Minister is the boss and can put a stop to the argument at any time he or she chooses.

CHAPTER FOUR

Building for the Government

In March 1963 there was not much time for such philosophical thoughts for a new arrival at the Ministry of Public Building and Works, a department which had just been created at extremely short notice by Mr Macmillan without any consultations with the Ministers affected. This was a Prime Ministerial decision with a vengeance. I don't think he had the slightest idea of the professional complexities involved. But if he did, he no doubt thought that sorting this out was what officials were there for.

The Minister, Geoffrey Rippon, set up a Reorganisation Steering Committee consisting of six officials with me in the chair to recommend the basic organisation and principal procedures of the new department so far as works and supplies were concerned. (This rightly excluded the Ministry's work on Ancient Monuments and Historic Buildings, which constituted a largely separate operation and which, under Edward Muir's authoritative guidance, had come to enjoy a high reputation.) The Minister, using his prerogative, gave us three months to do the job and instructed us to report by the end of June. This was indeed a challenge, but it was well judged. A shorter time would have been quite impracticable. A longer period could have left more time for argument.

And argument there certainly was. Traditions and procedures of each of the four constituent elements differed widely and none was the same as those of the Ministry of Education. I was appalled by the attitude of the Ministry of Works administrators towards the architects and their professional staff. These were regarded as a lower form of life: indeed, in much earlier years the architect concerned was not allowed to accompany an administrator to Buckingham Palace to advise on work there as he was not considered to be a gentleman.

The nature and extent of the problem of co-ordination was summed up in the introduction to the report:-

> The merger brought together four works organisations of markedly different character. In some, on the professional side, architects predominated; in others engineers. The relationship between professional men and administrators differed. So did the attitude towards delegation of both work and financial responsibility to outstations at home and overseas . . . Outside headquarters the organisations had little in common; the geographical lay-outs seldom coincided, nor did the arrangements for controlling new works, maintenance, employment of direct labour or the site control of major projects. Moreover, many of the differences were the result either of long tradition or of recent decisions taken in the full knowledge of possible alternatives and we were soon made aware that on a good number of issues rival views were strongly held . . .The differences were, perhaps, more numerous than the similarities. To find the best set of answers is a task of some delicacy, for our proposals will work efficiently only if the staff have confidence in them and we are conscious that our terms of reference bring us up against some of the problems which have been the subject of debate inside and outside government for many years.

However, the steering committee were determined to get unanimity and our report was produced in time. Edward Muir thought well of it and the Minister approved it. All that remained was to make it stick. It would be stupid to pretend that all was plain sailing. But civil servants are realists and they recognise when decisions are unalterable.

Relations between the Directorate-General of Works (the professional staff responsible for these programmes) and the newly-formed Directorate General of Research and Development under the architect Sir Donald Gibson were, however, another matter. Gibson, who had been the City Architect when Coventry was rebuilt after the war and County Architect of Nottinghamshire when his staff designed the primary school which won the top prize at the Milan Triennale, came out of a very different architectural stable. He arrived in the new Ministry from running the War Office Works Organisation, into which he had imported a style and approach very much like that of Hertfordshire in school building. This introduced a professional dichotomy between DGRD and the Directorate-General of Works under its Controller-General Sir Cecil Mant, which eventually proved not to be sustainable. The resolution of the problem in 1967 was as hard to face up to as anything in my eleven years as a Permanent Secretary. But it was worse for the loser.

Cecil Mant had had a career very different from that of Donald Gibson. As a very young man he had joined the Office of Works at a quite extraordinarily low salary. The civil servant authorising his appointment minuted 'His drawings seem adequate.' He then quoted the salary proposed and added 'No indication of any increase in salary should be given.' Times were tough in 1928. He had worked his way up to the top of the professional tree in Whitehall. He was a big man with a dominant personality. He was the man for large-scale projects. As fate decreed, the requirement for the biggest of them all arrived on our doorstep from the Admiralty on the very first day of the new Ministry's existence. It was for the multi-million pound Polaris base at Faslane in Scotland. (The Admiralty later confessed to us that they could not have tackled it under the old set-up for, in spite of the undoubted quality of their engineers, they did not have the variety of resources needed for so large and complex a project.)

We were very conscious that the eyes of the Admiralty (who had nominated a Rear-Admiral to look after their interests) would be upon us. So would those of even grander folk, for the construction of the base was vital to the security of the country. Cecil Mant took the project in hand and, to his great credit and that of his colleagues – and the satisfaction of the Admiralty and the Navy – ensured that the work, much of it highly technical, was completed on time and with no escalation of cost, other than that caused by inflation.

Meanwhile Donald Gibson and his group were hard at work partly on new developments and partly on projects that they had started at the War Office before the merger. At a grand parade at Gibralter I had much pleasure in handing over to the Governor the new barracks, strikingly situated high on the Rock, which were to be named after him – the Lathbury Barracks.

The large overseas element in the Ministry's programmes was fascinating in its diversity of buildings and climatic conditions – a new High Commission building in Islamabad, an army camp in Hong Kong, an airstrip and small harbour on the island of Masirah off the coast of Oman, a desalination plant in the Gulf, schools for the services in Malta and Singapore, a power plant (large enough to supply a town the size of Harlow) at Aden, a new Army camp in West Germany and electrical equipment for the dug-outs in the front line during the 'confrontation' in Borneo. All these at least got the Permanent Secretary out of the hair of his staff in London.

One of my visits was in support of Richard Sharples, then the Parliamentary Secretary and later so tragically assassinated when he was Governor of Bermuda. On arrival at the small airstrip in Salalah in Oman the young RAF flight lieutenant in charge boarded the aircraft and said to Dickie Sharples, 'I think I ought to warn you, Sir, that the guard of honour here is a little different from what you were accustomed to in the Welsh Guards. You will see that they are drawn up in a single line and as you approach they will fire off individually a *feu de joie* with live ammunition.' 'What do I do then?' asked the ever-polite Sharples. 'You walk along the line, shaking each man by the hand and say as near as you can get to in Arabic "May Allah be with you!"' The Parliamentary Secretary carried it off as though it had been part of his training at Sandhurst.

A special word of praise should be given to the wives who served overseas. They had married their husbands thinking of the Civil Service at home. To serve overseas (which neither they nor their husbands were compelled to do) might seem attractive – at any rate in some locations. But to live, as they had to do, in a senior military community accustomed to high-level hospitality and with its own distinctive protocol could seem a little frightening. In some locations there was danger too. Shortly before I arrived in Aden the wife of the Regional Director had seen, spattered over a wall near her house, the remains of a terrorist whose bomb had gone off too soon. She and other wives were a great credit to the Home Civil Service.

All this represented for the Permanent Secretary and his senior colleagues a tremendous challenge in management. But in spite of the frustrations and complexities we were all involved together in a creative venture, more easily identifiable as such than parts of the Civil Service such as the Inland Revenue or the Customs and Excise. For the Minister there was less attraction. He was present at such special occasions as the opening by Her Majesty the Queen at the Royal Aircraft Establishment at Farnborough of the vast new indoor test-bed for the hull of Concorde and by the Prime Minister of the Post Office Tower in London, two of the Ministry's most spectacular – and successful – projects. A Minister could also sometimes speak with great experience of the world on a management matter. For example, when I proposed to promote to a very senior post someone who had much capability and charm but lacked a certain amount of drive Mr Charles Pannell said 'I shouldn't do that. Never make a natural Lieutenant a Captain.' Not an easy management lesson to learn, but he was right.

However, politically, the post did not have much sex appeal and even in its enlarged state the Ministry ranked low in the political hierarchy. The Minister was, however, responsible for relations with the building and building materials industries and this gave him – and his Permanent Secretary – a 'card of admission' into some of the more central economic discussions in Whitehall. Among Ministers we had what I suppose the organisers of Wimbledon would call one 'wild card' entry. This was Miss Jennie Lee (later Baroness Lee of Asheridge), the widow of Aneurin Bevan. She was, as it were, parked out in the Ministry in order to produce a White Paper on the arts and, as a Deputy Secretary then, it was my job to help her. From inside the department we had the assistance of an Under-Secretary, Mortimer Bennitt, from outside in Whitehall Robert Armstrong, the future Secretary to the Cabinet, who was then based in the Cabinet Office, and – most important of all – she had at her elbow the formidable and talented lawyer Arnold Goodman (now Lord Goodman), who was made chairman of the Arts Council and has since performed such prodigies on behalf of the arts.

If there was humour in the Ministry it was to be found in Jennie Lee's office. 'I,' she told me, 'am the Duchess of the Labour Party.' It must have been the first – and last – time in history that when the Parliamentary Secretary to the Ministry of Public Building and Works rang the Prime Minister he stopped what he was doing and answered the telephone. She liked banter. It occasionally took her fancy to come to the office in the morning in a low-cut dress with a striking piece of jewellery around her neck to emphasise the effect. I said to her jokingly, 'You are not supposed to come to the office dressed like that.' 'Why ever not?' she replied. 'The Ministry needs a little cheering up.' Finally she took her White Paper, as procedure requires, to the Cabinet before publication. 'How did you get on?' I asked. 'No problem,' she said. 'I gave those boys a good talking to.' The Cabinet conclusions recorded that the White Paper was approved. Rather like the technical education White Paper nearly ten years earlier, it was a 'tract for the times', especially as the amount of new money that the government were prepared to make available was very limited. The only specific increases were a rise in the Exchequer grant to the Arts Council from £2,150,000 in 1964–5 to £2,815,000 in 1965–6 (both excluding Covent Garden) and an increase in the purchase grants to local museums over the same period from £54,000 to £108,000. An additional subvention to help the major symphony orchestras was promised once a committee under Mr Goodman had reported.

'Words,' say the cynics, 'cost nothing,' but the White Paper did contain a very useful and quite comprehensive survey of the current situation and the future prospects. It announced that responsibility for the arts at government level was to be removed from the Treasury and transferred to the Department of Education and Science. The White Paper also laid special emphasis on the encouraging developments in the schools and on the developing possibilities of television which, unlike radio, had barely begun to show what it could do in the field of the arts. The third aspect, on which Miss Lee herself was particularly keen, was the need to counteract the excessive concentration in London of the best in the arts and of expenditure on future developments. She therefore emphasised the need for much greater activity in the provinces and by local authorities in particular. Finally, she was anxious that solemnity should not be such a prominent feature of places like museums and galleries. 'More and more people,' said the White Paper, 'begin to appreciate that the exclusion of so many for so long from the best of our cultural heritage can become as damaging to the privileged minority as to the under-privileged majority.'

It would be going too far to claim that the White Paper had started a national revolution in favour of the arts, but it did create a mood and help to encourage constructive developments. The extent of the advance achieved can be gauged by looking back twenty years to compare the very different scope and style of provision for the arts today with that of 1965. One of the most notable differences is in the financial contribution from the private sector. This had been touched on only lightly in the White Paper, not for doctrinal reasons, but because we failed to appreciate the extent to which the business world could be persuaded that its long-term commercial interests might be served by greater sponsorship of the arts.

The second half of the 1960s was not the most exhilarating period in British economic history. Mr Wilson had enlarged his modest 1964 majority by a correctly judged opportunistic election two years later. But the country's relative economic position in the world had begun to deteriorate significantly and warnings about our loss of international competitiveness had become more frequent. No decisive action had, however, been taken to reverse it. Mr George Brown's National Plan had proved to be a failure, mainly because it involved an unrealistic amount of central direction and over-precise targets. This failure unfortunately gave planning of all kinds a bad name, so that it became impracticable to establish the kind of relationship that MITI and Japanese industry were already forging.

In industry there were some successful British firms who occasionally won a prize for, for example, the best-managed company in Europe. But it was noticeable that British managers tended to be more successful abroad than at home. With a Labour government in power this was the day of the trade union barons, who were skilled at identifying their bargaining objectives and at achieving them in long beer-and-sandwiches negotiations at No 10. Full employment was maintained at the price of a loss of international competitiveness, which could be masked only temporarily by devaluation of sterling.

In the construction industry this debilitating process was less obvious owing to the lack of competition from imports, and the industry built up an excellent record of success abroad. Even in the mid 1980s the construction engineering industry was producing a favourable annual trade balance of £1 billion, to offset in part the £2 billion deficit incurred by the rest of industry.

The educational policies of the Labour government did little to contribute to economic strength. There was some tendency to favour social engineering at the expense of the quality of education. The almost fatal failure to join the EEC when it was created in the mid 1950s could not be remedied ten to fifteen years later owing to the continuing intransigence of General de Gaulle, and so the spur that that might have supplied was not available. The only bright spots were that inflation was reasonably under control and that our invisible exports, resulting mainly from the activities of the City of London, were buoyant and growing. The government increasingly gave the electorate the impression that they had run out of ideas and it was widely expected that the election of 1970 would be a fairly close-run thing, even with a new Tory leader in the shape of Mr Edward Heath.

Meanwhile on a part of the economic front relatively (but not entirely) remote from these grander considerations the development of the Ministry of Public Building and Works was proceeding. So far as the industries were concerned, the advantage of practised personal relations showed itself once again. Manoeuvre accepted as part of the game, but always against the background of the integrity that alone breeds mutual confidence. Within the department, gradually improving integration of people and procedures and more confident relationships with the client departments. A few lighter moments, two of them sparked off by the presence of Field Marshal Lord Templer, trained in the Brigade of Guards, as Constable of the Tower of London.

We had met years before in Germany in September 1945 when

I accompanied Ellen Wilkinson as her Private Secretary on a visit to Berlin and parts of West Germany. Two flamboyant personalities, they had enjoyed themselves from the start, Gerald Templer opening the exchange good-humouredly by referring to himself as 'this obviously Fascist general'. (It was on that visit that at a military lunch Ellen Wilkinson addressed her brigadier host throughout the meal as 'Captain'. When I got near her afterwards to explain she said, 'Oh hell! I only know the ranks in the Fire Service.')

In the mid-1960s the Field Marshal, who was very commercially-minded, discussed with me whether we could create in the Tower a special 'Judgement Room' containing the axe and the block and so on, for admission to which we could charge extra. He was concerned that the Tower had (surprisingly) no rack and was delighted when he was offered one from Germany.

But this very modern Field Marshal decided that its age must be established by a carbon-dating test. This revealed that it was a nineteenth-century imitation. So the Tower of London did not get its rack and, as far as I know, has not got one to this day.

On the way back from this meeting I gave him a lift to the West End – and received a magisterial rocket in the process. While the new Knightsbridge Barracks were being designed by Sir Basil Spence, I went to a ceremonial dinner with the Royal Engineers at Chatham. My neighbour was General Sir Charles Jones, a former Engineer-in-Chief. 'Did you know,' he asked, 'that the plans for the original Barracks had been approved by the future General Gordon of Khartoum, who was a sapper? Would it be possible to arrange for these plans to be deposited in the museum at Chatham?' I thought that this was a good idea and arranged for it to be done. General Jones' letter of thanks included the fatal words, 'The whole Corps will be grateful to you.' I knew from this that I had done something wrong, but couldn't figure out what it was. In the car with Gerald Templer the explanation suddenly hit me. I thought there was nothing for it but to come clean. So I told him the story. 'You bloody fool,' he said (but amiably). 'You know who occupies that barracks. You should have given the plans to the Guards.' I was suitably contrite, but so far as I know the plans are still at Chatham.

In 1967, a more sombre duty. Although the merger was steadily maturing, there was one major problem. The tension between DGRD under Donald Gibson and DGW under Cecil Mant was increasing rather than diminishing owing to their very different personalities and approaches to architecture. It became clear that Gibson or Mant had to go, leaving the other in charge of all the professional staff in the department. This view was shared by my senior colleagues, and the Minister approved the proposal that the job should go to Gibson.

I asked Cecil Mant to come to see me. He knew that the decision would be in favour of a merger, but hoped that he would be chosen as head of the combined organisation. It was all the harder for him to accept that he was to be the loser. We spent three quarters of an hour together, and he behaved with great self-control. He said, 'I suppose there's no appeal?' I replied that he could certainly see the Minister, but I told him that I was afraid there was no possibility of the decision being reversed.

In spite of the intractable nature of the problem, I felt, as a manager, a sense of failure at having allowed this situation to arise. So it was specially pleasing that Cecil Mant subsequently achieved two remarkable successes on major projects outside government. The huge Barbican project had got into a mess and Cecil was engaged by the promoters to be their representative and to sort out things with the architects and builders. Which he did. He then performed the same function for the promoters of the new Covent Garden Market south of the Thames.

I was impressed by this technique and in later years persuaded those responsible for the extension and major refurbishment of the Royal Opera House to use the same technique. This was not immediately popular with the architects selected to design the project, but they soon came to recognise the benefit of having the users' requirements articulated by someone whose language they could readily understand. The young structural engineer concerned, Mr Robin Dartington, recruited from the National Building Agency, was a great success. It was largely due to this technique that the first phase was built with very little increase (except for inflation) over the sum set in the original appeal. Mr Dartington has continued to perform the same function for the second phase of that major undertaking.

It is very difficult to be a good client. Most people employ architects only once in their lives and naturally don't know how to go about it. The Hertfordshire school architects, with their close study of function, were very good at bringing the best out of their clients. It seems a pity that the Royal Institute of British Architects has never induced anyone to write a book entitled *How to be a Client*. Much time and money could be saved and much frustration avoided and better building should result.

By this time, after some twenty years' experience of architecture, building and planning, I had formulated a personal philosophy on this group of subjects. There was an opportunity to express it in a speech in 1967 to an audience of American architects gathered in New Orleans.

> 'A country's buildings,' I said, 'are the physical expression of the character of its people. As Sir Winston Churchill said "We shape our buildings and afterwards our buildings shape us." What do our present buildings tell of our humanity, of our intelligence and foresight, of our sense of beauty, of our desire to serve all of the people all of the time?
>
> 'We ought to consider more fundamentally what kind of organisms cities and towns really are, why they flourish or die, why some contribute more than others to social enjoyment and cultural vitality, and how to plan so that growth and re-development can occur without ruining the environment or bankrupting the community. I suggest too that we should study more professionally how to resolve the conflict between traffic and the human need for repose. One thing is vital – we must be so organised that we can see the picture as a whole and act accordingly. In Europe at any rate there have been too many cases in which the planning of transport has not been properly co-ordinated with the rest of urban design. And there are too many examples of cities with what I call hard, unwelcoming centres. The planners have not sufficiently studied what activities make a city centre live. Sometimes they seem to have forgotten that people are equipped with legs and hearts and not just with four wheels and a mechanical engine.
>
> 'My own feeling is that when we fail it is often for lack of softness and of contact with nature. I believe that these are fundamental human needs. When I am at my desk I can sit for quite a time concentrating hard on the other person or the papers in front of me, though even then I like – and I am fortunate to

have – restful colours, good pictures, well-designed curtains and a piece of sculpture.

'But sooner or later I want a pause. I want to walk around and look out of the window. Of course I am lucky because I have one of the finest views in Britain, aslant across the river to the Houses of Parliament, and Big Ben. But wherever I work I hope I shall always have a view of trees, grass, flowers and water. It is not, I believe, a coincidence that many of the environments generally held to be most satisfying contain at least one of these elements prominently featured.

'I do not say the same about main traffic arteries in cities, where the price of land is usually an almost overriding consideration. Along these arteries the faces of buildings can be hard and severe, though still I would hope beautiful and with enough of a three-dimensional quality about them to allow for the play of light and shade on the elevation, for to me this is part of the attraction of nearly all well-loved buildings.

'But I do make a plea that the spaces between the traffic arteries should provide the kind of environment I have described, with a human scale and an atmosphere that encourages repose.

'In the midst of all the problems that I have been discussing stands the architect, for not only does he design the buildings and play a main part in planning the cities, he is a principal trustee of the visual values of a community. His is a challenging profession, for he must be part creative artist, part historian, part technologist, part man of business, part psychologist, part organiser and part servant of the public. He lives in a world of choices and decisions, many of which demand sensitivity and mature judgment. Most buildings are no longer simple, materials are multifarious, and all the time advancing technology treads upon his heels.

'No longer can he build a career on an inherited store of architectural concepts. He must widen the base of his inspiration. It may come from the nature of the site – how many opportunities in school design have been lost by architects who have summoned a bulldozer and slapped the buildings down in a sea of asphalt! Or inspiration may come from the answer to a structural problem or even from the needs of such a prosaic maintenance task as the cleaning of windows. Above all perhaps it may come from a close and sympathetic study of the client's needs.

'I have finished on this theme because I strongly believe that buildings are not for the greater glory of civic leaders or architects or professional administrators and cities are not Utopian exercises for planners. Buildings and cities are for people. If we keep this in the forefront of our minds we shall not fail.'

CHAPTER FIVE

Trade and Industry

Early in 1968 Mr Robert Mellish, the Minister of Public Building and Works, whose robust common sense was a pleasure and whose political skill within the Labour Party an education, told me, just before the news was given to me officially by the Head of the Civil Service, that I was to become Permanent Secretary to the Board of Trade in succession to Sir Richard Powell, who was leaving before retiring age to become a merchant banker in the City. The President of the Board was Mr Anthony Crosland.

This switch left me only a total of two and half years as Permanent Secretary of the Ministry of Public Building and Works. By 1968 the merger of five years earlier had been largely successful, our relations with user-departments were in good shape, and massive programmes of new building and maintenance had been satisfactorily implemented. In this last respect we made greater use of private architects than was generally appreciated: at any one time they were busy on about £100 million worth of work for us (£750 million at 1989 prices). But we could not yet claim to have achieved adequate cross-fertilisation between the many different interests and skills in the department.

Recruitment of professional staff was the main outstanding problem. This problem was not limited to the Ministry of Public Building and Works and it was discussed, though mainly in the important but narrow context of improving career opportunities and achieving greater flexibility within the Service, in the Foulton Report on the Civil Service in 1968. The difficulty was deep-seated. It could not be solved simply, as some thought, by setting up an *Ecole Polytechnique* and throwing the higher posts in the Civil Service effectively open to professional staff. The solution needed educational reforms ranging much wider than a single institution, the creation of working conditions which would give professional men an adequately creative job in their early years, the formation within the Civil Service of more teams of mixed skills, the provision of opportunities for – and training in – management at not too late an age and a realisation that in the later stages there should be several different types of work available for professionals, all of them with an increasing management content.

The main thing was – and is – to get more professionals of good quality into the Service, otherwise they would, among other things, be overshadowed intellectually by the administrators and this would have bad effects on both. If one accepts that administration in the Civil Service is some kind of a profession, it is unrealistic to expect either administrators or professionals to be supermen in the sense of being able to master two professions – though I have known some administrators who thought they could! What can be done is to ensure that by working closely with professionals from their early years administrators can learn enough to enable them to play an effective part in management and the formation of policy in the professional sphere. Professional men, on the other hand, will have their hands pretty full during the latter years of their education in learning to be good professionals in the narrow sense. They too, however, can be helped to play an effective part in the management and formation of policy later on by learning a bit more about management during their education and by being given practical opportunities to learn more about it as their career proceeds. Both administrators and professionals need *ad hoc* training in management at some stage during their careers.

The work of the Ministry of Public Building and Works brought the Permanent Secretary on to several central economic committees, and I had had a good deal of experience, from youth onwards, of travel to foreign parts and had done some government business with other countries. But these two qualifications, even when supplemented by a reputation for energetic innovation, did not make me an automatic choice for the Board of Trade and the appointment came as a surprise to me and to the civil servants in that department.

The office that I inherited and was to occupy through many vicissitudes for the rest of my Civil Service career had one of the best views enjoyed by any Permanent Secretary. It was on the top floor of the rather military-looking building at the Parliament Square end of Victoria Street. Two of the walls consisted almost entirely of windows and gave me an unrivalled view across Westminster School to the Houses of Parliament. It contained a very large desk (constructed, I thought, rather too much like a barricade) with a conference table at the far end and in between some easy chairs for informal discussions by three or four people. In keeping with my army training I attached great importance to ensuring that all the most senior staff, who met there every Monday morning, were informed about all the major activities of the department. Some civil servants, perhaps particularly those brought up in the Treasury, consider that being a Permanent Secretary is a skill readily transferable from one department to another. This certainly applies to some of the work such as relations with Ministers and Parliament, and management of staff; but however able the senior staff are and however keen the Permanent Secretary is on delegation some knowledge about the department's fields of activity and contacts is essential. To think otherwise is rather like assuming that a good managing director of one firm will necessarily make a good managing director of another. Finally an incoming Permanent Secretary must establish a good rapport with his senior staff and make himself acceptable in their eyes.

So for the first few months after moving to the Board of Trade I used to spend most afternoons away from my office visiting each of the divisions (such as industrial and commercial policy, overseas trade, regulation of monopolies and mergers, iron and steel, chemicals and textiles, economics and statistics). On each visit I first had a talk with the Under-Secretary in charge and then went round meeting every member of his or her staff. The same applied to the out-stations such as the Companies Registration

Office, the Patent Office, the National Physical Laboratory and the Government Chemist.

The Board of Trade, originally an august body, which included such unlikely grandees as the Archbishop of Canterbury, had not met for one hundred years and the President constituted a quorum of one. As a rough generalisation it was concerned in 1968 with all the commercial terms on which British interests, particularly private interests, traded at home and abroad. Its special expertise, which was considerable and internationally respected, was in overseas trade. The civil servants dealing with it were, as a group, probably the most efficient practitioners of inter-governmental negotiations in the Civil Service. With some logic the Board had in the mid-1960s taken over responsibility for shipping and aviation, and there was the usual problem (not limited to the Civil Service!) that the Board of Trade regarded their new partners as Johnnie-come-latelys and the shipping and aviation people tended to regard their new department as old-fashioned and much too conservative. This last view was shared to an important extent, so I was told on appointment, by the Prime Minister (a previous President at the youthful age of thirty two) and by Mr Anthony Crosland, the President at the time of my arrival. Indeed the frequency of Mr Crosland's telephone and other contacts with his academic friends at Oxford and elsewhere was taken to indicate a loss of confidence in the department. So there were clearly not going to be too many feathers in the bed for the Permanent Secretary.

As in most other departments, most of the staff were engaged in work of an executive character – either approved trade policies or export promotion (in partnership with the businessmen who constituted the British National Export Council) or providing services such as the Export Credits Guarantee Department, the Coastguard Service or the Air Traffic Control Service. But for the smallish group of administrative staff a general economic background, acquired either formally through education or by long experience, needed to be combined with an experienced appreciation of the realities of business life. The former provided a sort of touchstone, to which those who possessed it could relate many of the issues that arose. Most of my new colleagues had it and so did Mr Crosland. I did not, and after a few months the word went round: 'He is not an economics man.' But I did set myself to learning. (He who loses the will to learn sets a limit to his achievements – and perhaps even to his life.) And my colleagues were generous in their help. Prominent in this process was my Second Permanent Secretary, Max (shortly afterwards Sir Max) Brown of New Zealand origin, to whom I came to owe so much in the rugged experiences of the next five years. My fairly extensive knowledge of industry and of businessmen, however, did something to redress the balance and my efforts to integrate shipping and aviation more fully into the department had some success building on the skilled work of the other Permanent Secretary, Sir David Serpell, who eventually went on to become the distinguished Permanent Secretary of the enlarged Department of the Environment.

The Board of Trade were great believers in the ineluctable pressures of economic influences. Central to the policy of successive Presidents was belief in the importance of the GATT (the General Agreement on Tariffs and Trade) forged imaginatively in the immediate post-war years. At the heart of it was the economic principle of comparative advantage. (Each country doing what it can do best and exporting the surplus to pay for imports.) Those who believed in the GATT saw protectionism as a natural national instinct when a particular industry was under threat through cheaper and/or more efficient similar products made abroad. But they rightly realised that to indulge this instinct was to provide only short-term relief because it fosters inefficiency, raises costs, narrows the consumer's choice and burdens those industries which are not protected. Indeed, it may make the ultimate rescue of the industry that is protected more difficult and sometimes even impossible.

This is, however, a description of an ideal world. Such perfection was not to be expected and the creators of the GATT realised that there would be a number of defensive arrangements by individual countries or groups of countries. The great thing was to keep up some momentum towards freer trade. On tariffs the negotiations in the Kennedy round in the early 1960s significantly reduced the general level of tariffs and a further marked reduction was achieved in the Tokyo round some twenty years later. As a result the tariffs of industrial countries now average only 5 per cent. Non-tariff barriers, including the general extension beyond goods into services, were harder to tackle, but some progress was made. Of course there would be occasional back slidings, sometimes of major importance, but a main virtue of the GATT had been to constitute a *general* pressure on countries to behave in a way that international economic good sense demanded.

All this involved the Ministers and officials of the Board of Trade and its successor departments in long multilateral sessions of tough and detailed bargaining, often exchanging a concession on one type of goods for a benefit on another. This was street-trading at government level elevated (usually after midnight) to a game of poker. It was valuable in itself, but it was also good practice, including good linguistic practice, for future membership of the EEC.

Perhaps too few people realise that since the Second World War world trade has been the main engine of economic growth. Whereas there has been a four-fold increase in world output, world trade has increased eight times. Not so many people remember that in the early 1930s a lemming-like resort to protectionism led to a reduction in world trade of about 30 per cent in just a couple of years.

Sometimes a relatively modest proposal to restrict imports could cause great concern because if it were implemented it would not only be damaging in itself but might spread to other products. In the late 1960s the United States and Japan became locked in a fierce tussle about textile imports from the latter to the former. The intensity of the struggle, which eventually involved meetings between the American President and the Japanese Prime Minister, was out of all proportion to the size and nature of the economic problem. In money terms Japanese sales of textiles and clothing to the United States in 1969 were only about 4 per cent of Japanese production and, more importantly, only about 1 per cent of American production. However, exports to the United States from the yet lower-cost sources of Hong Kong, Korea and Taiwan were about the same size as Japanese imports.

The GATT authorities were naturally concerned about this quarrel, but they were even more concerned when it threatened to involve other products and other countries. In an attempt to mediate and, in particular, to stop the dispute widening, M. Olivier Long, the Director-General of the GATT, called a conference in July 1970 in Geneva. It was attended by the Americans, the Japanese, the United Kingdom and the then six members of the EEC. There were the usual informal preliminaries – private talks between various of the parties and later some informal negotiation. Also, as usual, the times of the meetings were fixed to take account of the different time-zones in which the various countries were situated, so that telephone consultations could, if necessary, take place on any new proposal.

The Director-General of the GATT took the chair at one end of the U-shaped table. Ranged along the window side on his left were the EEC representatives (including the talented Ralf Dahrendorf, with whom I was later to have so many dealings when he became Director of the London School of Economics and Political Science). Facing them were the Japanese (on the chairman's right), the British (led by me) and the Americans. Behind us were the interpreters. At one session, when the Japanese delegate began to speak, the whole EEC delegation suddenly seemed to spring to life. This was puzzling. I realised only too well that I was new to such a scene, but I could not think why what the Japanese representative was saying was so important. It turned out that my puzzlement was misdirected. The attention of the EEC delegation had been seized not by the words of the Japanese delegate but by the appearance in the interpreters' box behind him of the prettiest Japanese interpreter seen in Geneva for years.

Simultaneous translation is a remarkable skill, even when one makes allowances for the lack of originality of many of the speeches. The more experienced delegates would sometimes enjoy themselves trying to defeat the interpreters. I remember one such British delegate on another occasion deliberately saying 'We intend to hit this proposal for six.' Unfortunately I don't recall what the French interpreter made of it. There was a time when General de Gaulle insisted that if no simultaneous translation were available every speech should be translated into French. One French delegate disapproved of this excess of patriotism and ostentatiously read a copy of *The Times* while the translation into French was being delivered.

The Geneva talks did succeed in helping to prevent the spread of the dispute beyond textiles. But though the atmosphere of the discussions was good-humoured, our attempts to get agreement on a regime for textiles based on 'voluntary restrictions' of exports or on the formation of a new GATT working group for textiles were not successful. The parties agreed to reconvene the conference if there were a prospect of positive results, but this never happened and the problem returned to being a bilateral struggle of considerable intensity. Both President and Prime Minister were involved again before an agreement was finally achieved between the two countries in 1972. The gladiators were not to know that this agreement coincided with the start of a period during which Japan steadily lost her comparative trading advantage. Indeed, in 1976 she joined the United States in complaining about the increasing threat of imports from less developed countries!*

Mr Crosland was not, I found, an easy man to read. What, for example, would his attitude be to a proposal to regulate conduct in the jungly world of take-overs by going for a City Take-over Panel and Code based on self-regulation by the City rather than control by law? Somewhat to my surprise, he agreed to the self-regulating approach and sent me off to negotiate it with the Governor of the Bank of England and other leading personalities in the City.

Under its formidable chairman Lord Shawcross, a former Attorney-General and the chief Allied prosecutor in the post-war trials of the Nazi leaders, the Panel got off to a very authoritative start. Some of those called before the panel told me, with post-prandial exaggeration, that they felt as though they had been in the dock at Nuremberg. Control was firmly established. The wisdom of appointing Lord Shawcross became increasingly

*For an extended account of this conflict see *The Textile Wrangle* by I. M. Dextler, Haruhiro Fukui and Hideo Sato published by the Cornell University Press in 1979.

apparent when in later years aggression and ingenuity combined to make effective control harder to sustain, particularly by those who had made their careers in the 'Square Mile'. This did the City's reputation no good and brought take-overs dangerously towards the legal and political ground that the original concept had been designed to avoid.

Before his departure Mr Crosland told me that he felt much closer to the department and, in spite of one or two unsatisfactory incidents, was pleased with the way things were developing. Not so the Prime Minister. It is sometimes said that past Presidents of the Board of Trade tend to have a love/hate attitude towards the department. If this is so, Mr Wilson in 1969 was certainly at the beginning of a 'hate' phase. On arrival at Torquay for a fortnight's holiday I was called straight back to Whitehall to be told that quite important areas of work were to be transferred from the Board to other departments, particularly the Departments of Employment and Technology.

Mr Roy Mason succeeded Mr Crosland for what turned out to be less than a year – not time for many important decisions; but one that gave him some satisfaction was the siting of the new National Exhibition Centre for Industry. For some years it was widely assumed that such a centre would find its home in London, perhaps at Crystal Palace, but the LCC and other interests never succeeded in putting together a convincing proposal. Birmingham did. There was some hesitation, I seem to remember, about 'the lack of night life' in Birmingham, but the proposal was soundly based and promised to be run by experienced managers. The access by road was first class and the small airport could be extended. So approval was given and Mr Mason's hopes for the project were realised.

Early in 1970 the Prime Minister turned his guns from the department to the Permanent Secretary on the grounds, surprising to me, that my style of management did not result in sufficiently tight control over the work of my subordinates. It was a mark of his disapproval that, as I learnt from a prominent industrialist, he decided that after the forthcoming election I should leave the Board of Trade. I think I know who fed the

Prime Minister with information hostile to me but the man is dead and I do not wish to criticise him when he is no longer there to defend himself. Depressing to say the least. But, as this narrative has already shown, the wheel of fortune can turn unexpectedly, and not always to one's disadvantage. The Tory success in the election of 1970 marked the turning point.

In opposition the Tories, advised in particular by one of the most distinguished retired Permanent Secretaries, Dame Evelyn (later Baroness) Sharp, evolved a new pattern of large departments linked with Mr Heath's desire to have a small Cabinet. One of these was to be the Department of Trade and Industry embracing the Board of Trade, the Ministry of Technology (which included energy policy) and the Ministry of Aviation Supply. As I later discovered, Dame Evelyn strongly recommended that I be appointed Permanent Secretary.

The departments were to be 'organised by reference to the task to be done or the objective to be attained'. On the industrial and commercial front this required the creation of a single Department of Trade and Industry. Its remit would be 'to assist British industry and commerce to improve their economic and technological strength and competitiveness'. The DTI was to become responsible for trade policy at home and overseas; marketing, investment and manufacture; design, research and development; service as well as manufacturing industries; public as well as private industry; and, of course, such matters as company law and the regulation of competition.

Mr John Davies (later Lord Harding-Davies) was to be the Secretary of State. He would be helped by three Ministers (each with the same senior status as Ministers in charge of departments not represented in the Cabinet) and three Parliamentary Under-Secretaries. Mr Davies had come new into Parliament after being the Director-General of the CBI. In that capacity he had dealt the Labour Party some pretty hard verbal blows; so they broke with tradition by heckling his maiden speech. He had a pile of notes on the despatch box from which he was, in fact, reading, which a Member is not allowed to do. A Labour member rose to his feet. 'Is it in order, Mr Speaker, for the Secretary of State to read out his speech?' Mr Speaker, anxious to give John Davies a fair start, replied, 'I did not think the Rt. Hon. Gentleman was reading his speech. My impression is that he is simply drawing heavily on his notes.'

The size of the DTI was not exceptional. It did not compare with the Ministry of Defence, the DHSS or the Departments of the Environment or Employment. In any event, out of a total staff of 26000, 17500 were engaged in providing separately managed services such as the Air Traffic Control and Safety services, the Patent Office and the National Physical Laboratory.

The main challenge lay in the very wide policy scope of the department and this challenge was focused in the perennial question of civil servants in this field to incoming Ministers: 'What have you in mind when you use the term "industrial policy"?' Mr Heath's answer was unhesitating: 'Disengage from industry.' In so far as this meant getting rid of as many controls and advisory councils as possible and reducing central planning to a minimum, the message was clear.

The vision was clouded, but not much, by the simultaneous injunction 'Act like Great Britain Limited'. It was explained that this related to our dealings with overseas competition. This was specially relevant to very big projects such as the development of a major new coal-fired power station at Castle Peak in Hong Kong. In that case only one British firm, GEC, was involved as a contractor and that enabled the department to give uninhibited help. The company were impressed by the work of John Lippitt, the civil servant concerned and, although he was a high flier, the Minister of the day thought (correctly) that it would be right to allow him to leave the Civil Service forthwith on transfer to GEC as their export co-ordinator, a post that he has filled successfully to this day.

But 'disengagement' did not include, for example, ducking out of dealing with monopolies and mergers and the Heath government were no more prepared than was Mrs Thatcher's later to dispense with such aids as regional development assistance. Moreover the defence procurement programmes were always going to be influential in their effect on the structure of important sections of British industry. Overshadowing these items was the government's firm determination to get Britain into the EEC.

This would inevitably involve many close and continuing contacts between government and industry, whether opportunities or constraints were in question. And, in relation to nationalised industries Ministers faced the long-standing challenge of how to combine adequate freedom of action for management with adequate control of public expenditure.

Unfortunately, in my view, the phrase 'industrial policy' has got itself the status of a slogan, as though it were some well-defined approach with which one either agrees or disagrees. The fact is that every government has to have an industrial policy of some kind, even though a Tory government may feel happier with a phrase such as 'policy towards industry' rather than 'industrial policy', just as under Mrs Thatcher the government has preferred a policy about incomes to an incomes policy. Mr Heath's White Paper seemed to me to have phrased the objective correctly by talking about the need to 'assist British industry to improve its economic and technical strength and competitiveness'. It would have been helpful if this had been firmly reinforced by a determined drive in education to produce more and better young people qualified to perform adequately in the circumstances that the White Paper described.

Whether under a policy of disengagement or the opposite, one of the most demanding tasks for senior civil servants is to advise Ministers on what to do about a 'lame duck' firm. Just as protectionism represents a sort of knee-jerk reaction to the failing international competitiveness of an industry, a major firm threatening to go bankrupt is liable to provoke heavy political pressure for help, especially if several hundred jobs are at stake. In those circumstances it is the duty of the Civil Service to provide a clear-headed objective analysis of the firm's position and prospects and for the senior officials – and usually the Permanent Secretary himself – to see that that view is fearlessly presented to Ministers. It is for them to judge whether political considerations outweigh economic and financial judgement; and if this causes the Permanent Secretary problems in his personal capacity as Accounting Officer direct to the Public Accounts Committee, the approval of the Prime Minister and/or the Cabinet can over-ride his judgement. The best advice to Ministers in these circumstances is to try so far as possible to swim with the economic tide rather than against it.

The new department had its critics of course. Some of them were businessmen disgruntled by individual decisions or disappointed because the DTI failed to espouse particular causes. But the greatest irritation arose because of the difficulty in gaining acceptance, in both Parliament and the business world, of the need for the Secretary of State to adopt as determined an attitude towards political delegation as was more easily achieved at the official level. Gradually, as the new arrangements matured, the Ministers – who were, after all, of Cabinet rank – came to be accepted as tackling on a delegated basis some four-fifths of the work for which they were responsible. This allowed the Secretary of State to reserve himself for the really big challenges.

The biggest challenge of all was entry to the EEC. The Cabinet were determined upon it. So, in particular, was John Davies. So, as it happened, was I; but it would have been my duty to work for it and to see that the Department worked for it to the best effect even had I myself not been convinced. By 1970 the government's view was quite widely shared in both Parliament and industry and, as the national referendum later showed, by the electorate. But a great deal depended on what terms we could get. One thing was certain: we did not see ourselves as a 'Little Britain' going into a continental grouping in order to keep warm, so to speak. There would be no ready-made radiators in the Common Market. We saw membership of the Community as a great economic opportunity – and perhaps over-rated the comparative industrial strength of the UK in the process.

The Common Agricultural Policy was regarded as an extremely sensitive subject and when the Foreign and Commonwealth Office agreed to my supplementing the efforts of Ministers with a short tour of several of the European capitals in order to gather informal views on trade and industry they particularly stressed the undesirability of mentioning the CAP. I dutifully complied with this request – and was amused when in each of the capitals concerned the officials whom I met said, 'You haven't mentioned the CAP. What are you planning to do about it?' 'We are still thinking about that.' 'Well you must do something. It is absolutely terrible.' A different comment would, no doubt, have emerged if I had been allowed to extend my tour to include Paris.

The Commonwealth needed some reassurance about the possible effect of our joining the Community. Some of the concern was general. The Canadians, for example, needed to be reminded that even when we became members we would be trading with them on a large – and probably increasing – scale. The Australians had been more specifically sensitive: for example the anxieties about the effect of our joining on the canned and dried fruit producers, many of whom were ex-Servicemen. But during the 1960s the general Australian attitude towards our bid for membership had become steadily more relaxed. Like the Canadians, however, they wanted to be reassured about our intention not to weaken our links with them. As part of our efforts in this direction a visit to Australia was arranged for me. The 'natives' were very warm in their welcome and it proved helpful to have been in the desert with the Ninth Australian Division under command during the Battle of Alamein – some good-humoured 'joshing' about which had been the more memorable: the performance of the Aussies against the enemy during the battle or their exploits in Cairo afterwards.

At that time the Sydney Opera House was being built – marvellously impressive when seen from a customs launch in the harbour. At a lunch afterwards organised by the Australian/British Trade Association I thought it would be tactful – and also truthful – to make a complimentary comment on this remarkable structure. From the far corner table among a fairly large audience came a shouted Australian intervention: 'You can take it home with you if you like!' On my return to London, Sir Charles Johnston, the British High Commissioner in Australia, kindly sent me a copy of his report to the FCO on my visit, which he judged to have been 'a considerable success'. I was especially flattered to read the comment of one senior Australian: 'That is the most unstuffy Pom I have ever met.'

Membership of the EEC was clearly not going to do us much good unless the momentum of change in the UK could be maintained. This depended fundamentally on political will. But the Civil Service also had a contribution to make – a reminder, once again, that knowledge of the art and science of change-making is an essential part of any good senior official's equipment. Another requirement is that civil servants should always try to see how a situation looks from the point of view of the 'prime movers', the people who are trying to get things done. One should consider, as it appears to them, the accumulation of controls. These controls may each seem quite satisfactory individually, but how do they look when they are lumped together? A Grand National is stimulating once a year, but not every day.

This is one of the ways in which the skills required of civil servants differ from those needed by most businessmen. To put together a policy for a whole industry – or group of industries – involves more complications and wider issues than is common in a business. In a business there are the central touchstones of the balance sheet and the profit and loss account and the desirability of creating viable profit centres at various levels to which decisions can be delegated. The risk that a civil servant runs is to be seduced into introspection and unreality by the complexity of the problems. That is an important reason for making sure that civil servants maintain close contact with the outside world and for reminding them constantly that they are scene-setters, one of whose most important functions is to create the conditions in which other people can do their best work.

It is easy for a civil servant to forget that he or she is a servant of the public as well as of the Crown, government and Parliament. 'A little brief authority' may be a necessary ingredient, but a helpful attitude is even more important. This applies especially to the executive functions of a department. The public who come to a department for some service, some benefit or some permit or simply some information are easily frustrated. It is up to the management of a department to see that the staff are good at putting themselves in the shoes of their 'customers'. This requires continuing effort.

A civil servant is much more comprehensively accountable than his opposite number in the private sector. The Parliamentary

Commissioner for Administration (the Ombudsman) is a fairly recent innovation. The work was skilfully started by Sir Edmund Compton in 1967 and the independence and integrity of the Commissioner's investigations (at the instance of MPs) have been well maintained. More formidable – because it is more intrusive – is the work carried out on behalf of the Public Accounts Committee of the House of Commons by the staff of the Exchequer and Audit Department (now called the National Audit Office). Too few people, perhaps, understand that a small group from that department sits in each major government department, day in and day out, and can send for any files at any time – except those on which replies to its queries and enquiries are being drafted.

It is the reports from these groups that are used by the Comptroller and Auditor General to provide potential material for his annual reports to the Public Accounts Committee. These are serious and professional affairs. The reports are directed not at the Minister but at the Permanent Secretary as 'Accounting Officer' responsible for the efficient and economical use of money and people in the department. The committee is chaired by a senior Member of the Opposition – usually a former Treasury Minister – and the members are people of quality and experience. The C&AG's report would cover such matters as a bad over-shoot on costs incurred in the construction of an army camp at Aden, the problems of Rolls-Royce when it had been nationalised or a more general subject such as the efficiency of the development of nuclear power stations.

Such an occasion concentrates the mind wonderfully. It is a very personal affair. It is also liable to be full of technicalities, with some of which one may not be familiar. There is not much consolation in the fact that, owing to the lapse of time, one quite often finds oneself discussing actions taken under one's predecessor. The discipline is very salutary but, perhaps unfortunately, the reports of the PAC seldom have much political sex-appeal. So the House as a whole usually takes little notice of them. The Accounting Officer used, I believe, to be liable to the limit of his personal fortune (or some such phrase) for any financial shortcomings; but as it is very many years since any

Permanent Secretary could qualify as the possessor of a fortune that threat at least was unreal.

Though the PAC mount investigations in some depth, the most formidable enquiry is one by a tribunal set up by the Home Secretary to enquire into a 'definite matter of urgent public importance'. A tribunal of this kind was appointed to investigate the collapse of the Vehicle & General Insurance Company, for a short time the largest motor insurance company in the country. Because it was an insurance matter it was a responsibility that the DTI had inherited from the Board of Trade. The tribunal consisted of a High Court judge and two QCs, who later became judges, one of them, indeed, a Law Lord. The counsel to the tribunal was also a future judge, so was the DTI's counsel, and the British Insurance Association was represented by Lord Elwyn Jones, a former Lord Chancellor. All this considerable legal talent imported the atmosphere of a court of justice. It was later considered to be a disadvantage that the tribunal contained no retired civil servant who would necessarily have had a more informed knowledge of the working of a government department than a group of lawyers however distinguished could gain by the most skilful investigation. The tribunal that was appointed some years afterwards to investigate the short-comings of the Crown Agents, who purchased goods on behalf of a number of British Colonies, decided to draw a clearer distinction than did the V & G Tribunal between the enquiry phase needed to inform the tribunal and the phase in which a witness became, in effect, a defendant against a charge.

In the V & G case the issues were difficult and delicate: difficult because of the complex nature of the job of monitoring the affairs of insurance companies (particularly those set on a course of fast expansion) and delicate because precipitate public action by the department might well have caused the premature collapse of the company. The question at issue was whether anyone at the Ministry had been 'negligent' in the technical sense by failing, in lay language, to perform up to the level of professional skill and judgement that he might be expected to have.

Inevitably the report of the tribunal was critical, but we were all dismayed when they found that Christopher Jardine, the

Under-Secretary in charge of Insurance and Companies Division, was guilty of negligence. We thought that he was vulnerable to a charge of misjudgement, but not one of negligence. However, there was nothing for it but to advise the Home Secretary and the Prime Minister that the findings of such an influential tribunal should be upheld. But we did arrange for Jardine, with Sir Ashton Roskill's goodwill, to be found a job in the Monopolies Commission, which he performed satisfactorily until his retirement a few years later.

The tribunal's proceedings lasted for some time, during which I aimed to make an appearance for an hour every afternoon in order to demonstrate the interest and concern of the management. I was of course also required to give evidence, partly about organisation and procedure in the department as no one above Jardine had been involved in the case and partly because the tribunal wished to make up their minds whether I had been negligent. They decided that I had not.

Some years later after the annual dinner that the de la Rue Company give at the Dorchester to the Diplomatic Corps and to some of the allegedly great and good in British public life, I accepted the usual invitation to go up to the terrace at the top of the hotel for a final drink. By a remarkable coincidence the only three other people in the lift were Lord Elwyn Jones, Lord Justice Templeman (a member of the tribunal) and Sir John Arnold (counsel to the tribunal), all of whom had had a go at me when I was giving evidence. In the way that lawyers have, they each greeted me warmly and to the following effect: 'My dear chap, how nice to see you! I have never enjoyed myself so much as that afternoon that I cross-examined you.' That, I thought, doesn't make four of us!

Tribunals are, fortunately, pretty rare. Select committees of each House of Parliament are a more regular feature of the scene. Some select committees have existed for many years. But it was not until Mr St John Stevas, as Leader of the House of Commons, announced in 1979 that each government department would be brought within the ambit of a select committee that a more effective system of monitoring started to emerge. The Public Accounts Committee had always been authoritative, but it was concerned essentially with investigation after the event – sometimes quite a long time after the event. The new select committees have served two useful purposes. The first has been to sharpen investigations by the House of current- or more nearly current – issues and so to subject the government representatives to a more considered investigation than is often practicable, at least at Question Time and in Adjournment Debates.

Sometimes the questions of select committees lead – deliberately – into areas that are commercially confidential and might make public price-sensitive information. With good sense on both sides serious clashes can usually be avoided, but very occasionally the temperature is raised especially high and I have even known one MP threaten to move that a Permanent Secretary be committed to the tower for contempt of Parliament. (This tower, is, by the way, not – as one might suppose – the Tower of London, but the Victoria Tower at the southern end of the Houses of Parliament.)

No less important than the impact on Ministers and officials is the impact on the Members themselves. Because a Member has to be something of a jack-of-all-trades to his constituents the number of subjects on which he can be an expert is limited. Sometimes, indeed, his knowledge of a subject does not go far beyond Party slogans. So the chance that membership of a select committee provides to get more closely acquainted with the work of a department (or group of departments) can be very valuable not only to the MP (and therefore to the House of Commons) but to the department because it thus acquires a wider informed constituency.

The attitude of officials at meetings of select committees – and indeed of other committees – is very important. It should be as helpful and forthcoming as circumstances allow. But civil servants do have to learn one technique because on most occasions journalists and sometimes broadcasters are present. This is the technique of avoiding the instant quote that could damage the Minister or the department. There is often pressure for senior civil servants to divulge what advice they gave to Ministers. If this were done a fatal Rubicon would be crossed. The position of the Minister as head of the department would be impaired and the civil servant would become a more public (and probably more party-political) figure than would be healthy under the British constitution – or for his employment under a government of a different political colour.

Nowadays many senior civil servants – and Permanent Secretaries in particular – are expected to do much more public speaking than would have been thought right in the 1930s – to professional institutions, business audiences (large or small), conferences, prize-givings, etc. Some of this is serious stuff in the form of papers that are published afterwards.

In such cases officials must be quite sure that their remarks represent the views of the government of the day. If there is any doubt in their minds when the speech is being prepared they should submit any sensitive point for prior approval. Such speeches are permissible because Ministers do not have enough time to accept all the worthwhile invitations that they receive and are well content that those civil servants whom they know to be adept at public speaking should cover some of the ground. Needless to say, an official should never accept an invitation to address a party political audience.

One other contribution that a senior civil servant can usefully make, if he is inclined towards it and can get good at it, is after-dinner speaking. This minor social craft can provide some useful lubrication and generate goodwill. It can also show sometimes sceptical audiences that civil servants are really quite human beings! You have to learn the rules, of course. Research carefully your audience and their likely interests. Never speak for more than twelve minutes (or fifteen if you are absolutely sure that you and your material can hold the audience's attention that long). Don't attempt to make more than three points of substance. Try out the precise wording in your bath – the punch-lines must come over to the best advantage. Get the audience on your side as quickly as you can and don't be humorous at the expense of the previous speaker. Try to get a really good laugh in the first two minutes. It is best if this is *not* done by means of a funny story, particularly if there is a risk that some of your audience may have heard it before.

Sometimes a useful piece of relevant information comes to one's notice by coincidence. One came to me from reading the *News Of The World* in April 1970 shortly before the 'Saints & Sinners' dinner, where many journalists would be present. This was the longest newspaper headline that I had ever seen. It was followed by a brief story, which bore out every word: 'Nudist welfare man's model wife fell for the Chinese hypnotist from the Co-op bacon factory.'

For a Permanent Secretary contributions to communications outside the department are much less important than communications within it. Like all other heads of departments I saw my Secretary of State pretty well every day. Being familiar with each other and with most of the issues that arose these meetings usually lasted for less than half an hour. Mr Walker thought it particularly important that his Ministers should think and act as a team. He therefore had a daily meeting with them on their own. For some reason best known to themselves, the press reported that I had strongly resisted this proposal. But this was quite untrue. I told Mr Walker that I thought it a good idea.

Both Mr Davies and Mr Walker gave much attention, with me, to the development and co-ordination of policy and information. A department's policy stemmed in part from the Party Manifesto and in part from the continuing experience of the department. However, there was no single document in which the various strands of the policy were drawn together. The momentum tended to be provided by the legislative programme, the general intentions expressed in the Queen's speech, the execution of policies already announced and the impact of external events.

In the DTI we thought that something more was required, so we imported into the department the technique that I had used during my time in charge of technical education. Every six months we issued to all the senior staff a document entitled 'Policy Developments'. In the light of government policy and the known wishes and ideas of departmental Ministers, it began with a statement of about a dozen general objectives. It then listed the principal policy developments of the previous six months. Finally it set out those policy developments ('major' and 'minor' in separate sections) which were intended to be brought about during the following twelve months. This document was compiled by the Central Secretariat (headed by an Under-Secretary) under the direction of the Top Management Group (a body of about ten top officials which met weekly under my chairmanship) and it was of course submitted to the Secretary of State and his Ministers for approval.

In addition to policy developments we issued a weekly circular for senior staff (*DTI This Week*) giving information about the main policy matters currently under consideration by Ministers and top officials and news of parliamentary matters of concern to the department. We also prepared a regular – and excellent – newsletter about EEC developments, which was circulated to other Departments as well as our own. In addition there was a brief Information Bulletin, issued weekly, giving news and forecasts of matters of interest to the press. Finally, we started a departmental newspaper entitled "*TIE–Line*" (modified to *TI-Line* when the Energy group had been separated from the DTI) which was circulated to the whole of the staff. It was in tabloid form, like a newspaper that I had started in MPBW and which still survives in the Department of Environment. *TI-Line* also survives under the title nowadays of *DTI News*.

We were trying to create a department with a style of its own, compatible with other departments but with, we hoped, some useful innovations. All this activity arose primarily because of the size of the department and its considerable policy interests (there were over seventy Under-Secretaries). Our aim was 'to establish a balanced and responsive organisation, adaptable to changing circumstances, able to handle effectively both strategy and tactics in conditions of heavy pressure and fast-moving events and capable of attracting the continuing loyalty of those who serve it.'

The style of the department was important. In the hundredth edition of *DTI This Week* I wrote:

> So what precepts does my personal experience prescribe for the management of the DTI? Go for quality wherever it is to be found and get the right mixture of skills. Strive to be clear, practical and

> simple: people who make things sound complicated have often not understood them well enough. Avoid Parkinson like the plague.
>
> Identify your objectives with care and spend time on telling your colleagues what they are. Delegate to your staff and trust them – and support them when they are in trouble. Establish a sense of success and have as good and quick a system of two-way communication as can be devised, both inside and outside the department.
>
> Above all perhaps, encourage a broad outlook and never let the Department become introspective. Get out of your office as much as you can. Stay close to the realities of industry and commerce, always maintain an international perspective and give pride of place in your thinking to the needs of the 'customer' in his or her many manifestations.

In trying to 'stay close to the realities of industry and commerce' what did we find? In commerce, we saw the City of London in good shape, at that stage pre-eminent internationally and contributing invaluably to invisible exports and so (usually) making the country's over-all balance of payments tolerable. Competition and the advance of information technology had not yet induced the City to be as innovative as it could have been and in some operations large commissions too easily earned were no spur to action. This condition led many years later to a slowness to appreciate the full implications of the changes which led to the Big Bang of 1986.

These handicaps were, however, remediable. They were less serious than the inadequacy of the links between the City and industry. The relationship between those who financed industry and those who managed it was too slender and often too temporary, unlike the long-term interest of German banks, which provided most of the funds for German industry. The increasing pressure on the City fund managers for short-term results (sometimes very short-term) made it then – and still makes it now – more difficult than it should be to build bridges of understanding between industry and the City. Nevertheless, had industry been as internationally competitive as the City, the United Kingdom would have been a good deal more prosperous than it was.

The DTI's relationship with the City was essentially regulatory and, except for the direct supervision of the insurance world, much reliance was placed on the use of intermediate bodies – the Office of Fair Trading, the City Take-over Panel and the Monopolies Commission. The Treasury, of course, dealt direct with the Bank of England and the merchant and clearing banks. The DTI's most direct contact was ECGD's work in the field of export credit insurance, which had a good reputation. Ministers were not much preoccupied by relations with the City, except that occasionally, when a take-over was involved, the heavy political artillery might be wheeled into place, especially if a large number of jobs was at stake.

Retailing required rather more supervision, particularly in the field of prices and consumer protection, but the main development, which took place independently of Whitehall, was the growth of the really big retail groups who could use the weight of their large-scale buying to make goods cheap to the customer. This activity started a revolution, as a result of which the smaller firms and the village shops had to fight for survival. The big increase in mobility because of the considerable rise in the ownership of motor cars helped the revolution along. With the exception of Marks & Spencer, who bought British and exercised close control over their suppliers, the big retail groups did not hesitate to go abroad in search of value for money and this led to a sizeable increase in imports. Of course some of the goods could not be produced at home. At lunch one day with a trade association I sat next to the managing director of a big chain of wine merchants. 'What is your most profitable line just now?' 'No doubt about it,' he replied, 'Chateau Plonk,' and unnerved me slightly by his description of the size of the tankers in which the wine was transported around the country for bottling. That marked the start of another major revolution – the development of Britain into a wine-drinking country.

Manufacturing industry was a different matter. Its problems were the central preoccupation of the DTI. Mr Heath's injunction to 'disengage from industry' could be interpreted as implying that if the government were to get off industry's back all would come right. But it was not as simple as that.

Industry as an organism was not healthy. It had been beset for many years by its social inheritance and it had become something of a battlefield on which the champions of two opposing social and economic philosophies had sought to further their cause. Even a strong organism would have found it hard to prosper in such a swirl of controversy, about the desirable extent of nationalisation, the role of competition (national and international), the part to be played by government in regulating and restructuring industry, the scope for planning and the proper role of the trade unions. All these factors brought to bear upon industries wrestling with change and modernisation had imposed on them a heavy handicap. There had been neither a national consensus nor a consistent policy.

These shortcomings were due in part to industry itself: for individually successful though many firms had been, the management of industry had failed to formulate and secure convincing collective policies, partly because it had not spared enough effort for the task and partly because it lacked the sanctions that were available to the trade unions on the one hand and to governments on the other. It had also not succeeded in attracting its fair share of the national talent or in stimulating the development of enough good engineers at all levels. Successive governments, we thought, should also admit to some of the blame. In some cases they had not had a sufficiently close understanding of the problems of industry. But their main short-coming had been not to give a high enough priority to industry's needs when these were in conflict with other objectives – economic and social.

This consideration highlighted the responsibility of Treasury officials for knowing enough about the problems and opportunities of industry to get an accurate perspective, for – as the Board of Trade had always been fond of pointing out – changes in macro-economic policy (such as the exchange rate, interest rates, the degree of inflation and the level of public expenditure) could affect industry more than any number of micro-economic measures. For this purpose it was specially important for Treasury officials, whose work did not naturally bring them into regular contact with industry, to get out on the ground and keep themselves up to date. Moreover, the customary token posting of a Treasury high-flier to another department for, say, three years was not an adequate substitute. As for the DTI, one of the purposes of having a really powerful department was to make it more likely that the Treasury would acquire an adequate industrial perspective. As things turned out, the department was in existence – in my day – for too short a time for this objective to be achieved, even though the Treasury made a real effort to widen the scope of their macro-economic consultations.

The lack of priority for industry proved to be a main drag on progress when so much of the change which was inescapable was bound to require substantial reductions in the size of the labour force in politically sensitive industries or locations. To remain efficient and competitive industry had to extrude many thousands of people from such activities as coal mining, the railways, iron and steel, textiles and ship-building, and the introduction of more capital-intensive machinery was bound to affect the livelihood of many more.

The natural resistance to these changes had been strengthened by the slow growth of alternative employment, and the lack of new investment had been compounded by the even more serious defect of failure in many cases to achieve a return on capital comparable with that of our overseas competitors.

Those who hoped that the working of a relatively free market economy buttressed by marked decreases in tariffs and the liberally conceived framework of the GATT would stimulate competition and national competitiveness enough to ensure relative success had been disappointed. So had those who put their faith in a greater degree of central control and a large increase in the size of the public sector.

It would, however, be wrong to imply that the whole picture was black. During the previous thirty years the UK economy had grown faster than at any other time during the last hundred years. The management of some leading British firms had been acknowledged by informed overseas observers to be the best in the world: so had their skill and that of their City advisers in organising expansion abroad. Over 90 per cent of British firms seldom had much serious trouble from strikes and in technological invention we had had notable commercial successes, such as float glass, nuclear fuel, diesel engines and medical electronics. Finally, the discovery and exploitation of North Sea oil represented a major achievement. Moreover, it was, perhaps, only through the retrospection that the Queen's Silver Jubilee encouraged that one appreciated the extent to which the general standard of living had increased.

So failure was relative. But that failure could prove critical if it resulted to an important degree, as it did, from low productivity compared with that of our main competitors and if this were accompanied by differentially high inflation. Looking abroad it seemed clear that success had come not so much to those countries which had followed a common economic policy but to those who had established the most enduring national economic consensus about industrial policy – witness the approaches, different in each case, of the United States, France, Germany and Japan.

Was there a chance of establishing such a consensus in Britain? Mr Heath's government hoped so. The trade unions were central to the argument. Powerfully led at national level by such people as Mr Hugh (later Lord) Scanlon and Mr Jack Jones they would either do a deal on a basis that could last – or not. The alternative seemed to be to continue through the years with the all too familiar swings and roundabouts. To the Tories another bout of nationalisation and central planning was, of course, anathema. On the other hand, they had not yet articulated a radical alternative, such as Mrs Thatcher and her friends produced later, which would involve 'moving the goalposts' and trying to establish a consensus on ground well to the right of what seemed practicable in the early 1970s.

In 1972 the government's main concern was about prices and incomes, which had risen by 16 per cent and 25 per cent respectively during the previous two years. But when the talks between the government, the CBI and the TUC began in March the Prime Minister set this central problem against the background of the efforts that the government had made to meet the TUC's suggestion about 'faster growth, lower unemployment, help for the regions, higher pensions, raising the tax threshold, cuts in indirect taxation and measures to hold down prices in the nationalised industries'. Mr Heath then referred to the price restraint programme instituted in July 1971 by the CBI.

The TUC, looking as ever for a potential bargain, introduced a proposal that the new Industrial Relations Act, which brought the possibility of access to an industrial relations court into the field of wage bargaining, should be abolished or suspended. The talks progressed only slowly and the sparring for an opening continued. Early in July the CBI were able to announce that 200 of their largest companies had agreed to continue the 1971 programme of price restraint until the end of October 1972 – but not beyond. The TUC countered with pressure to do something special for the lower paid.

After a high-level working party representing all three interests had tried to focus the arguments in a broad context, Mr Heath put forward to a tripartite meeting at the end of September detailed proposals for the following two years: a 5 per cent growth target, a limitation of retail price increases to 5 per cent over the next twelve months, a ceiling of £2 a week in the annual increase in pay for a normal working week and certain improved benefits for the low paid. The TUC countered with a detailed statement disagreeing with almost all the government's proposals to a greater or less degree. In particular they pressed their view that restraint on price increases should be made statutory, an idea that the government considered impracticable for any length of time ahead. The government retorted with a proposal that the limitation on wage increases should be backed by legal sanction.

It became apparent that a deal could not be struck and the talks ground to a halt in November. At the end of that month, as a temporary measure, the government imposed by statute a 'ninety days freeze' on prices, incomes, rents and dividends. It was, perhaps, unfortunate that these talks took place in the shadow of what became known as the 'Barber Boom' and the ultimate rise of inflation to a degree that was not only unhealthy in itself but raised the spectre of a failure to sustain the much-prized 'full employment'. In football terms one might say that the trade union representatives 'played for a draw' – and succeeded. All was not lost by the government, but not very much had been won – except, perhaps, that the talks had taken place at all.

After the 1974 election the Wilson government took up the theme of an industrial strategy. This was altogether a more ambitious affair than Mr Heath's tripartite talks. Some elaborate preparatory work and consultations were carried out before the government produced in November 1975 a White Paper entitled 'An Approach to Industrial Strategy'. This was discussed immediately before publication at a meeting of the National Economic Development Council held at Chequers. It contained a number of unexceptionable sentiments – the need to give in the immediate future priority to industrial development over consumption or even 'our social objectives, better co-ordination of government policies and matters affecting the efficiency of industry.' Also, a need to enable industry to earn sufficient profits, to have access to adequate sources of external funds and for better training arrangements: 'We must get away from policies of confrontation and work together in the national interest towards agreed objectives.'

As might be expected, the White Paper referred to the part to be played by the National Enterprise Board and Planning Agreements as well as to the less controversial Finance for Industry and the Manpower Services Commission. Recognising the excessive rigidities of Labour's National Plan of the mid 1960s, the government proposed instead a rolling sector-by-sector analysis based on systematic statistics and looking five years ahead in an attempt to identify 'those sectors which are likely to have most potential and those which may be expected to present problems.' At the same time the government recognised that "some of the biggest disparities in performance at present are found within particular sectors rather than between them'. The "Little Neddies" (the EDCs) would play an important part in the analysis and the recommendations for action.

Perhaps it is fair to say that the White Paper was an attempt to achieve a unity of approach by papering over the cracks of disagreements of long standing. But although the White Paper was not badly received, the prominence given to centrally-directed planning and – still more – to Planning Agreements and to a National Enterprise Board with a scope immensely wider than that of the Industrial Reorganisation Corporation and with statutory powers made it unlikely that effective co-operation would result.

Moreover, the White Paper was published soon after the most damaging increase in 1974–5 in average earnings by 28 per cent and average price increases by 25 per cent, and by 1976 the economy had deteriorated to an extent that required the intervention of the International Monetary Fund. The White Paper was quietly forgotten.

So we were back in the strategic log-jam. There were two ways to break it: the first on the initiative of government, the second on the initiative of industrial management. As for the first, the situation could be radically improved only if the Tories or the Labour Party could shift power, probably including legislation, so decisively in one direction that the shift would in practice be irreversible. This is what Mr Benn wanted to do in 1974 when he was Secretary of State for Industry. It is what Mrs Thatcher has aimed to do since 1978.

But these governmental actions would prove lasting only if they were matched by an initiative from industry itself. No legislative framework on its own would be sufficiently durable. Fortunately an initiative was available and some firms were already embarking on it. Its roots lay in history. Over the years the spread of education and the pervasive development of the media had led to strong pressures for social change in industry. These pressures had resulted partly in the growth of industrial power and partly in demands for greater accountability. The problem was how to reconcile the maintenance of enterprise with the aspirations for a fairer society which education tends to generate. These aspirations would continue to grow. Government and Management needed to respond to these pressures in ways which recognised that industry, whether private or public, was a competitive enterprise; for once the ability to compete was lost the spirit of enterprise was lost. And this would be true not only in the private sector but for much of the public sector as well.

Strong, professional and imaginative management was essential. However much management was hedged about with accountability its power to act must not be so constrained as to be emasculated. Did this mean, then, that the continuation of an adversary relationship within industry was inevitable? To this question many would answer yes, in times of peace. They would say that in wartime people voluntarily abrogated their self-interest, individually and collectively, in the face of an external threat, which they accepted as temporarily over-riding. By doing this they enabled to be forged a sense of commitment that was the key to success. The workers accepted more readily the dictates of management and they voluntarily suspended their accustomed rights of argument and veto.

The people who held these views argued that such conditions could not be reproduced in peacetime. They saw as insurmountable handicaps the unions' fragmented structure, their over-ready resort to restrictive practices and withdrawal of labour, their heavy-handed pursuit of narrow interests in pay negotiations and their failure to understand the imperatives of a successful business. These people did not believe it possible to secure any real sense of commitment. So their main aim was to conduct an adversary relationship with the minimum damage to the objectives of management.

This attitude might come naturally to some frustrated managers, but it contained within itself the seeds of its own destruction. It could lead only to increasing tensions and more frequent interruptions to production. On the other hand, it was no use trying to go to the opposite extreme of hoping for sweetness and light all round and a co-operative consensus on every decision. Against it were the facts of human nature, the pace of business life and the bargaining – sometimes tough bargaining – which were an inescapable part of that life. The need was to formulate a better and more constructive approach. The prize to be won was the positive commitment of workers and their unions to the success of the business. Their inherited perspective was too narrow and this was not their fault.

Traditionally the men and women on the shop floor had been closely concerned only with wages and working conditions. They had little knowledge of the rest of the expenditure and practically none at all of the income. They saw figures which gave them a broad idea whether a company had done better this year than last year; but in a company of any size these figures related mainly to the corporate result rather than to those of individual businesses, let alone those of individual units. 'Business reviews' were sometimes published alongside the formal accounts, but many managements did not make a very intensive effort to explain their significance. Moreover, in some cases the problem was made more difficult by the considerable size of plants in some key locations.

The frustration was liable to be increased by the fact that many people reached their maximum pay grading by their early twenties and had little prospect of further advancement. Finally, the trade union officials were relatively poorly paid and many were not capable of taking a broader view even if they had been inclined to do so.

The influences described earlier in this chapter were already beginning to make all these attitudes seem out-dated and would continue to do so in greater degree irrespective of the political situation. What was clearly needed was much more delegation by both management and unions. People needed to work in teams which meant something to them, in units the objectives of which they could understand and in whose success they could have a palpable share.

All this required a restructuring of many businesses into 'profit centres' closer to their markets and with considerable freedom of action within a given framework. In engineering this process was assisted by the need for more and more people at all levels to acquire skills wider than their original qualifications and, to use the jargon of the day, mini-production lines making complete components and manned by multi-skill workers. It was important that such people should no longer be faced by an employment dead-end in their early twenties. The way was opened too for younger managers with a more participative style than many of their predecessors. These changes, which had quite radical implications, could not be brought about simply by common sense and goodwill. Managers had to be trained in the new approach and to learn new techniques, often making use of more computerised systems. Many shop-floor workers needed to broaden their skills, often by straddling the boundaries between electrical and mechanical engineering in the process.

At first sight the unions had a problem. Delegation might erode the power base of the more senior officials, and the loss of traditional demarcations might have a powerful effect on the influence of individual unions. But there was another way of looking at it, and the arrival in the UK of a number of Japanese firms helped the process. One of the British leaders in developing this approach was Lucas Industries where, as a non-executive director, I was able to observe the pioneering work masterminded by Dr John Parnaby, the director of group technology. The favourable effect on production, morale and commitment was striking. With the new approach individual workers could be helped to be much more conscious of the performance of their section of a business. Some leading trade unionists began to appreciate that even if certain structural changes in the direction of plant or industry unions had to be made this was the direction in which success lay. This included the possibility of the members of Unions exercising a greater influence on the conduct of the business than had been the case up to that time.

A rearguard response action would threaten rather than help the well-being of their members and, therefore, ultimately of themselves. This consideration could not, however, be expected to prevent all rearguard actions, particularly in some of the nationalised industries.

New organisational arrangements and a leadership willing to consult and listen would be required: it was interesting to observe how few managers had the self-confidence to listen. But this would not suffice to produce a sense of full commitment. Money needed to be part of the equation. This would range from full profit-sharing for everybody to profit-sharing through increases in pay reflecting the profitability of each major part of the business linked with decentralised wage negotiations.

Instinctive political reactions to this scenario might suggest that it was a party matter. But the truth was that if international competitiveness were to be adopted as the main objective (as it clearly needed to be) there was no viable alternative to following this trend. Governments would need to understand that success could be achieved neither by a strong concentration on central planning nor by leaving everything to the working of the market. The former would run clean counter to the process of effective delegation and to the trend of society since the mid-1950s. The second would show an inadequate appreciation of the state of British industry when viewed in an international context.

International competitiveness proved to be an invaluable touchstone, especially for those relatively few firms on which the country's economic prosperity ultimately depends, partly because of their own size and partly because of their impact on their suppliers. It would not, however, be helpful to deduce from an analysis of this kind that a certain number and type of firms were essential to the economy or even that manufacturing industry should account for a given proportion of the output of the UK. International economic conditions changed with the years as the principle of comparative advantage developed. What promised prosperity for Britain in, say, the 1950s would not necessarily do so in the 1970s.

A constant attention to the demands of international competitiveness did, however, throw up the need for a continuing appraisal of the performances of our competitors – the equivalent in industrial terms of the work of an army intelligence staff in times of war. This was an activity that seemed to us – and seems to me still – to be underdeveloped. Many firms would do their own appraisal; but the government would often have a part to play. For example, defence procurement could greatly influence the development of an economy: witness the effect on American industry of the massive subsidisation by successive US governments of research and development in a defence context.

A different type of problem for government would be derived from, say, the automotive industry. How essential was it to the health of the British economy that it should include a major motor car industry and, if so, how important was it that that industry should be British-owned? Such a question had an obvious political relevance because of its effect on jobs. But more important still was its commercial relevance internationally. A government that favoured central planning would do such a study anyway, but it would need to take into account *all* the relevant considerations and not just employment. A government that preferred to rely on the working of the marketplace would also need to do such a study, if only because they would have to be able to take part in realistic discussions with the firms concerned, and to be ready to consider whether, for example, to support their R & D and to condition their political supporters to back a particular solution.

Any government would also need to continue some support to export promotion. This would include trying to ensure that our diplomatic posts knew enough about the industrial needs and potentialities of the country concerned in order to advise and, if required, to help British businessmen in making the necessary contacts. This was particularly the case with big projects such as, a large chemical plant, a new airport or a new suspension bridge. Such major projects often also involved difficult questions about the terms on which credit should be granted to help industry win a competitive race. A competition of this kind was liable to hit the headlines and if the British firm lost out strident criticism would be liable to emerge in Parliament and the media on the lines that the UK government had failed to give adequate support to the British competitor.

For a government such a situation resembled the problems of how much to support a major firm that had got itself into difficulties at home or how much financial support to give to firms to establish themselves or to expand in the less favoured regions of the UK. Wherever possible guidelines had been established, but it would often lead to uneconomic expenditure of public funds if the maximum amount normally available for a project or type of project were to be made public.

A really big project would also tend to involve factors other than directly commercial factors; for example, did the government attach such importance to earnings from exports to particular countries either generally or for political reasons that it would feel justified in 'going over the top'. The French policy of *crédits mixtes*' (giving credit on particularly easy terms, sometimes with a grant thrown in) was quite often quoted against a British government. In cases of this kind governments were making an often difficult judgement whether or not it was worth putting up more than a particular amount of the tax-payers' money in order to subsidise a particular project.

On export promotion, during Mr John Davies's time, we made one organisational change which was not popular with a number of leading businessmen. The British National Export Council was a voluntary body of prominent industrialists who gave a good deal of their time to helping the export effort – for example in setting up a British Week in Stockholm or by establishing a committee called COMET to advise on trade with the Middle East. They were supported by a secretariat who knew what they were doing and with whom Whitehall had good contacts. But they could not, of course, be made privy to all the government's actions and negotiations *vis-à-vis* other countries and there was an overlap which was uncomfortable, though not – fortunately – in personal relations. This gave rise to a fair amount of frustration and inefficiency. Some rationalisation seemed inevitable. How to combine the strengths of the leading businessmen with those of the officials in Whitehall? The answer seemed to be to arrange for the businessmen as a British Overseas Trade Board to work directly with Whitehall without the BNEC secretariat.

This was not a very agreeable solution to propose, but after a number of discussions in which I was known to have been personally involved a change of this kind was proposed to the Secretary of State. He approved it in spite of the fact that by doing so he disadvantaged some of his former colleagues at the CBI. This decision aroused some influential opposition, but I was startled when the chairman of ICI (then chairman of BNEC) voiced his resentment at the decision on the occasion of the council's annual dinner when, perhaps relishing the attraction of the phraseology, he made to several dozen top businessmen the factually accurate but constitutionally improper comment that 'We were doing all right until Part did us death.' Fortunately the opposition to the change did not last too long, though there were naturally some individuals who were never really reconciled to it.

In those days the balance of trade tended to be thought of essentially as the balance between exports and imports of goods and services. The significance of physical investment overseas was thought of mainly as a useful contribution to 'invisible exports'. Its importance to international industrial competitiveness was, I think, under-rated. As more and more trade crossed frontiers it became natural – and sometimes essential – to support and supplement the export of goods by establishing a manufacturing base in the country concerned. For example, in the US a major American manufacturer might well not recognise as a regular supplier of components a firm that did not have a relevant manufacturing unit in that country. The same might be true for political reasons in the quite different circumstances of a country such as China.

Increasingly too scale became relevant. In an international context British industrial companies were often not strong enough in either money or skilled manpower to tackle a particular overseas market. So there was a growing need for joint ventures with a partner in the country concerned. One British firm could be involved in such joint ventures with several different partners in several different countries.

All this was essentially a matter for industry, although the overseas trade group in the DTI, embassies abroad and the Patent Office were quite frequently involved. When Britain joined the EEC close contact between government departments and the industries concerned became essential. This connection was most evident in the sphere of agriculture, but there were parallels in other industries.

These rather complicated inter-connections were well illustrated by developments in aerospace, responsibility for the civil aspects of which the DTI took over in 1971 when the Ministry of Aviation Supply was abolished. This work was supervised at Second Permanent Secretary level by Sir Peter Thornton, who was well versed in commercial matters and later became Permanent Secretary to the Board of Trade.

The airlines, the managements of airports, Rolls Royce (nationalised in 1971 following the failure of private enterprise), the rest of the aerospace industry and export promotion were all involved. This interlocking complex of interests illustrated well the advantage of having a department with fairly comprehensive responsibilities. The Ministry of Defence and the FCO would have been involved in any event; but before the DTI was created the Ministry of Aviation Supply, the Ministry of Technology and the Board of Trade would have made a difficult and contentious complex of subjects even more difficult and contentious to handle.

By 1970 international air traffic was growing apace and the airline and airport businesses were securing for Britain a good market share. But progress had to be maintained and a strong committee under Sir Ronald Edwards, a professor at the LSE turned businessman, and at the time Chairman of the Beecham Group, had delivered to Mr Crosland in 1969 a comprehensive and cogently-argued report on the whole subject of civil air transport. Among other important matters, the committee recommended that a National Air Holdings Board should be appointed to exercise financial and policy control over BOAC and BEA in order to increase the strength of the British base and to rationalise resources. There was the clear implication that the two airlines should eventually be integrated into a single operation.

Sir Ronald, who was sometimes known as 'the prophet of competition', also recommended that British Caledonian with British United Airways, both enterprises in the private sector, should be built up as a 'second airline' and that the British Airways Board should transfer certain important routes to it. The judgement of respective size was difficult and British Caledonian were naturally dissatisfied with their allotted share, but the arrangement worked out reasonably well. The problem was how to give British Caledonian a decent chance without handicapping British Airways in its competition with the most powerful airlines elsewhere in the world. The government had approved the report in 1970.

The airport business was more controversial. The demands on Heathrow were growing fast and seemed likely to continue to do so. It was already one of the biggest airports in the world, second only to O'Hare Airport in Chicago, and with one aircraft landing every minute in daylight. Apart from the need for additional capacity, aircraft noise was a problem. At one stage the inhabitants of Egham worked up a strong protest about the number of aircraft due to fly over them. Ministers agreed that their protest seemed to be justified and were minded to announce that a proportion of the traffic should be routed over more open country to the west of Heathrow.

This greatly reduced the number of people concerned but the views of some of them needed – and received – careful and respectful consideration. Among the few formal objectors were the Earl of Drogheda (then chairman of the *Financial Times* and of the Governors of the Royal Opera House, Covent Garden) and Sir Philip Allen (later Lord Allen of Abbeydale) then Permanent Under-Secretary of State at the Home Office. Lord Drogheda, whom I knew quite well, agreed to spend with me what turned out to be a fascinating afternoon in the country west of Heathrow with a noise-monitoring van owned and operated by the National Air Traffic Control Service. It would be going too far to say that he was satisfied, but at least he had acquired a closer understanding of the problem. Philip Allen, like the experienced civil servant that he was, knew when he was on to a loser and, being a polite man into the bargain, as well as a good colleague, did not press his objection.

The location of the third London Airport (Gatwick being the second) was an altogether more complex affair. A strong Commission under the Hon. Mr Justice Roskill was appointed to make a recommendation. To what extent should the prospect of quieter aircraft and ever more sophisticated arrangements for controlling air traffic be taken into account? Should the government's undertaking not to expand Gatwick by additional runways be abandoned with the certain prospect that there would be strong protests about the government's ill faith? What other locations were possible starters, bearing in mind not only the essential requirements for an airport (including air traffic control factors) but the possibility of adequate road and rail links to London?

The Roskill Commission relied heavily on a cost-benefit approach – some people thought too heavily because some of the costs and some of the benefits were not too easily quantifiable. They reported in 1970 in favour of Cublington west of Luton.

Needless to say, there were violent protests from some of the interests who would be disadvantaged and from other interests who strongly preferred another location. The government found the report less than completely convincing and decided in favour of another of the Roskill options a coastal site at Foulness in Essex; but this too was eventually not pursued.

The government did, however, press on – also in 1971 – in line with the recommendation in the Edwards Report – with the creation of a statutory Civil Aviation Authority. The government would remain responsible for policy, but the authority was to take over the economic and safety regulatory functions hitherto dispersed between the Air Traffic Licensing Board, the Board of Trade and the Air Registration Board. The authority would also be responsible for the civil side of the National Air Traffic Control services, for operational research, for long-term airport planning and for the main work of international traffic rights negotiation.

It was agreeable to read the committee's statement that: 'In the course of this enquiry we have seen a great deal of the civil servants in the civil aviation division of the Board of Trade. We have been impressed not merely by their devotion but by their shrewdness in business matters. The criticism that civil servants are too detached and theoretical in their approach and too little acquainted with the problem of the undertakings and industries they supervise is certainly not true in the case of civil aviation.'

Under its vigorous chairman, Lord Boyd-Carpenter, the new CAA got a good grip on its job and it took pride some years later in the historic ceremony at which the chairman handed over to Sir George Edwards, the chairman of BAC, the certificate of airworthiness for Concorde. There was one down-beat effect of the creation of the CAA. The staff side of the DTI were against it, mainly because it would move a good number of officials out of the Civil Service and would limit career opportunities, at least for those who were not professionals. The strength of their opposition put a stop for some time to further hiving off from the Civil Service.

The Concorde was a remarkable achievement technically and as a major Anglo-French project. International co-operation was nothing new in aircraft manufacture, but Concorde carried this process to unprecedented lengths. Differences in approach in many spheres have often hindered collaboration between the two countries, but in this case it worked, though at the expense of extending the time needed for development.

The decision to develop a supersonic airliner turned out to be a commercial mistake partly because no amount of commercial success could recoup the ultimate development cost of over £1 billion and partly because we failed to get permission from certain other countries to fly supersonically over their territory. Two of the most profitable routes would have been from London to Sydney and from London to Tokyo. As for the first, to our surprise the Australian government would not let Concorde fly supersonically over any part of their territory and thus cut the profitability and the competitive advantage unacceptably. The Tokyo route involved flying via Moscow and there were high hopes that this would be allowed, but we did not have available any quid pro quo (as was always required in the sphere of air traffic) that was attractive enough to the Soviet government to induce them to agree.

Even in the US Concorde was not welcome to everybody. There was, of course, no question of our being allowed to fly supersonically over American territory. This was not a problem for flights to New York and Washington DC. At the latter, however, the sheriff of the county into which the runway of Dulles Airport extended voiced the sentiments of a number of his constituents when he threatened to arrest Concorde and its crew if the aircraft ventured, as it inevitably would, on to that part of the runway that was within the boundary of his County. We thought that especially if the Sheriff were to elect to appear on horseback it would be the photo-call of all time, but Ministers did not want any incident and the sheriff was ultimately pacified.

For hot-weather trials before entering the service the aircraft was taken to California with Mexico City as the only intermediate stop. Afterwards the British Ambassador to Mexico enjoyed himself mixing the traditional with the very modern by 'having the honour to report' that Concorde, having left Heathrow on such and such a day at such and such an hour had arrived at Mexico

City on the same day at the same hour. To a layman even a short flight in Concorde revealed a new dimension. During the work-up period a small party of us led by Lord Carrington, then Secretary of State for Defence, flew south over the Bay of Biscay and then turned north to return to Britain. Because of the supersonic speed the diameter of the turning circle was ninety miles. Much nearer the in-service date, with a Labour government back in power, British Airways were busy training the cabin crew. Mr Gregor Mackenzie, the Minister of State at the Department of Industry, and a large party of us flew from Heathrow to Gander and back in a day (three and a half hours out, one on the ground, and three and a quarter hours back). On the way out the pilot had a good gag. Just over two hours out and halfway across the Atlantic, at the highest point of the flight, he announced, 'We are now starting our descent into Gander.' In spite of a little trouble with one of the engines on the way back, the greatest hazard of the flight was nothing to do with the flying. In order to practise the cabin crew in looking after real passengers we were expected to eat a full-scale first class lunch on the way out and another full-scale lunch on the way back.

In aerospace we were in among the big battalions so far as personalities were concerned. The chairman of the British Aircraft Corporation, Sir George Edwards, had a reputation stretching from the design of the Viscount through to Concorde. The chairman of Hawker-Siddeley, Sir Arnold Hall, made his name when he was Director of the Royal Aircraft Establishment at Farnborough by elucidating the cause of the tragic explosion of the Comet. This failure in a pioneering aircraft due to a relatively small fault in the window design was a tragedy not only in itself but in its repercussions, for if this first commercial jet aircraft in the world had succeeded and been profitable – as it well might have been – Britain might have snatched an invaluable lead in what amounted to a new era in commercial flying. As it was, the Americans – and particularly Boeing – walked away with it. Years went by before the Europeans could convince themselves that they had the will and the money to collaborate over a wide-bodied jet in the form of the Airbus in order to try to dent the American monopoly on large passenger-carrying aircraft which, unlike Concorde, had some hope of earning a financial return. What with civil airlines and military aircraft a great deal of public money went to the aerospace companies and the ability to lobby the government for money was almost as important for a chairman of such a firm as the ability to run the business.

In 1971 a third considerable personality came on the scene. Sir Kenneth Keith (later Lord Keith of Castleacre), then chairman of Hill Samuel, took on the chairmanship of Rolls-Royce when it was nationalised because it had over-stretched itself trying to develop the technically excellent RB-211 jet engine. For defence reasons alone no government could have contemplated letting the company go under altogether.

Controversy has raged for many years over the best way to run and supervise nationalised firms. Various ingenious ideas have been propounded. The National Economic Development Office (NEDO) produced in the mid-1970s a suggestion for a carefully balanced supervisory structure for each nationalised industry designed to establish a strategy to which governments, managements and unions would be substantially committed. But Ministers thought that such a commitment would be all too likely to be abandoned in a crisis, especially if a large number of jobs were at stake.

Ministers of both the main parties tended to think that the action most likely to lead to success was to appoint as chairman a major figure with a proven track record. This would often involve an appointment from the private sector. But the object would be not to import some powerful influence antipathetic to the objectives of nationalisation but to provide a leadership ready to accept the parameters of nationalisation, capable of working with all the interests concerned and with a distaste for failure.

This prescription was by no means intended to bar promotion from within the public sector. Indeed this had been done successfully on several occasions and it was desirable that good succession planning should lead to more of it.

Sir Kenneth Keith was certainly a major figure. Two years after his appointment by Mr Heath's government the Labour party returned to power and in 1976 the National Enterprise Board (a sort of Industrial Reorganisation Corporation, but with a much wider scope and statutory powers) was set up. Its chairman was Sir Don (later Lord) Ryder, Chairman and Chief Executive of Reed International. When this occurred Rolls-Royce were responsible in the first instance to the NEB. As can be imagined, there was a considerable clash of wills. This was not the kind of issue that a Secretary of State wanted to get involved in if he could avoid it, so the Permanent Secretary was detailed to sort it out. In this task I failed, partly because the department was itself an interested party with duties to perform in relation to the National Enterprise Board. So the procedural solution of the day was adopted. 'Ask Arnold Goodman to arbitrate.' This he agreed to do in spite of being ill and confined to his flat in Portland Place.

Each party was represented by two people. Sir Kenneth Keith and his deputy Sir William Nield, the former Permanent Secretary of the Department of Economic Affairs, sat together on one sofa facing across a low table Sir Don Ryder and his deputy Sir Leslie Murphy, also a former civil servant, on another sofa. A third corner of the square was made up by myself and my deputy David Jones on upright chairs. Facing us was a large armchair with an upholstered foot-rest in front of it. Arnold Goodman made his entrance in a pair of yellow pyjamas with a dark blue dressing gown and a pair of red slippers. He put his bad leg up on the foot-rest and the proceedings began. The best simile that I can think of to describe the nature of the discussion was that it was rather like a verbal version of Thai boxing, a quite alarming sport in which, within carefully prescribed rules, the contestants are allowed to kick as well as punch. In such a situation the weight of Goodman's influence had to be experienced to be believed. In the end he contrived an agreement that all three parties felt they could live with. The Secretary of State was, I think, relieved to be able to approve the solution.

Back in 1972 there had been a ministerial reshuffle. Mr Davies was made Chancellor of the Duchy of Lancaster and asked to spend most of his time on relations with the EEC. His knowledge of languages and his experiences at Shell, where he had first made his reputation, as Director-General of the CBI and then at the DTI, represented formidable qualifications for his new job. But he was sad to leave the Department that he had so recently created and nursed through its teething troubles. He was succeeded at the DTI by Mr Peter Walker, then only forty, who since 1970 had been Secretary of State for the Environment. He was very political (having been at the age of fourteen 'the youngest Young Tory in history') and having done well in business, mainly on his own account, he had a very ready understanding of commercial matters. On his arrival he immediately – and quite properly – said that nothing to do with Slater Walker should be referred to him. Would I please deal with anything that occurred in that connection? (As it happened the proposal to merge Slater Walker and Hill Samuel did crop up after a time, but it was not pursued.) One day – nothing to do with the merger proposal – I took Mr Slater out to lunch in order to get to know him; in the circumstances it would not have been appropriate to allow him to pay for a lunch for me. As things turned out, I didn't pay for the lunch either. The well-known restaurant concerned got so many things wrong (seven, if I remember) that they footed the bill themselves.

Mr Walker's commercial capabilities were specially useful not long after he took over from Mr Davies. Early in 1973 the British economy, not yet enjoying the benefits from North Sea oil, was greatly affected – as were those of other countries – by the decision of what became known as the OPEC countries, under the leadership then of the Shah of Iran, to quadruple the price of oil. Though the Shah had been complaining for some time about the inadequate prices received by producer countries in the Middle East compared with the price they were expected to pay for imports, his success in securing a combined decision from Saudi Arabia and his other neighbours came as something of a surprise in its timing.

While the government of the UK were assessing the prospective impact on the economy and what general measures needed to be taken, Mr Peter Walker got his colleagues' agreement to the negotiation of an ingenious and opportunistic deal with Iran. He personally settled the main outlines with the Iranians in London. They would sell to Britain in 1974 and early 1975 very large extra quantities of oil at prices a long way below the international market prices then ruling and Britain would sell in exchange considerable consignments of goods and commodities of which Iran was in need. We despatched Mr (later Sir) Peter Carey with a party of leading businessmen to Tehran to clinch the deal. He then accompanied Mr Walker to St Moritz to complete the agreement with the Shah at his winter holiday residence there. (This coincided with a visit by the Chancellor of the Exchequer who was discussing other business with the Shah.)

In the event Britain bought an extra five million tons of oil, which represented an increase of over 4 per cent in our total oil imports in 1973, and this amounted to an increase of 25 per cent in oil imports from Iran. The price fixed was just over $7 a barrel, which compared with a market price at that time of anything up to $17 a barrel. The exports connected with this deal, which were sold at attractive prices, were worth £110 million. They included petro-chemicals, synthetic rubber, synthetic fibres, paper, newsprint and steel. Peter Carey's success in the various phases of this important and complex mission did much to emphasise the strength of his claims to succeed me as Permanent Secretary three years later. This operation, in which the only other Departments involved were the Treasury and the FCO, was immensely less complicated than it would have been before the DTI was created.

Important though they were, joining the EEC, the broad issues involved in the relationship between the DTI and industry and commerce, developments in aerospace and the Iran barter deal accounted for only a small proportion of the work of the Department. The rest ranged from dealing with the traditional nationalised industries such as coal, steel and the Post Office, an electricity strike in which we set up 'operations rooms' in London and the regions to give advice to industry and the public, competition policy, relations with interests such as the chemical, textile and automotive industries, developments in computers, a range of measures in the sphere of consumer protection and the development of regional policies. We also moved the Companies' Registration Office to Cardiff and set up outside Newport on what must be one of the most attractive sites occupied by any government department a Business Statistics Office to serve both the government and industry.

All these and other activities placed a heavy load on the establishment staff led first by Mr John Leckie and then Mr (later Sir) Douglas Lovelock. Earlier in my career the job of establishment officer had not been highly regarded, but as the challenge of management came more to the fore the post rightly increased in importance. In any event, in creating and developing a department such as the DTI with component elements that came from quite differing backgrounds and traditions we needed people of high quality in that job. And we got them. One innovation close to my heart was to have in the DTI a full-time trade union adviser. Such an appointment could serve several useful purposes. If made – as it was – with the consent and advice of the General Secretary of the TUC it could strengthen the links between the department and leading trades union representatives. It could help Ministers of either party to get a deeper insight than some of them (even Labour Ministers) had into trades union attitudes towards particular problems. It would certainly teach civil servants more about unions, particularly as the Service tended to regard dealings with the unions (other than the Civil Service unions of course) as the private preserve of the Ministry of Labour. Finally, it might help the man himself to broaden his experience.

It was important that this man should not be seen by anybody as a spy in the camp and vital that this rather unorthodox appointment should have the whole-hearted approval of the Secretary of State, the Prime Minister and the TUC. The choice of the man was, therefore, crucial.

The name recommended to us was Ken Griffin, then secretary of the Welsh section of the Electrical Trade Union. He had the intelligence to do the job, an outgoing manner, a sense of humour – and, most important, the positive goodwill of the TUC. The appointment was made in 1970 by Mr John Davies and the fact that it was made under a Tory government came as a surprise to some trade union leaders.

Ken Griffin and I had a lot of talks together. He was brought up in Wales at a time when the ambition of many of the brightest

Welsh boys and girls was to go into teaching. Ken was very good at games. When he was fourteen his Headmaster sent for him. 'Griffin,' he said, 'you are spending too much of your energy on games. You had better get your head down and do some more work, otherwise – who knows – you might finish up in industry!' It was as well for us that he did. He filled the specification for our job admirably and succeeded in remaining *persona grata* with everyone inside and outside the department.

Around the turn of 1973–4 my Civil Service colleagues and I thought that the DTI had got over its teething troubles and was developing well. The department, under the leadership of its Ministers, had a good many achievements to its credit, and we had practical proof that the absence of inter-Departmental boundaries made for greater ease of relations, a shared general understanding, a more easily co-ordinated approach to policy issues and therefore for higher efficiency. We believed that costly though the implementation had been in terms of creative effort and hard work, the concept of the DTI had been vindicated and it had become an established part of the Whitehall landscape.

It was not to be. On the stroke of midnight on 4th March 1974 the telephone woke me from my sleep to receive some very bad news. Robert Armstrong, then Principal Private Secretary to the Prime Minister, was on the line. He informed me that to fit a particular pattern of new Ministerial appointments the Prime Minister was making for political reasons the DTI was to be broken up and divided into three departments – Industry, Trade, and Prices and Consumer Protection. Where, I asked, was Sir William Armstrong, the Head of the Civil Service? 'He has gone home,' said Robert. I was disgusted that William Armstrong should have ducked the job of breaking the news to me himself, but there was clearly no room for argument.

Robert told me that Mr Tony Benn was to be Secretary of State of Industry, Mr Peter Shore was to take charge of Trade and Mrs Shirley Williams of Prices and Consumer Protection. Robert added that I was to become Permanent Secretary to the Department of Industry with the nauseating rider that the Prime Minister wanted Mr Benn to have the best Permanent Secretary.

Would I meet Mr Benn at breakfast time in the department to discuss how the DTI should be broken up? This at least I was not going to have. I sat down there and then to work out a way of doing it.

This move was completely unexpected by the Civil Service. The customary warning at election time by the leader of the opposition to the Head of the Civil Service had not been given, so no plan for breaking up the DTI existed. But it was clear that the faster we moved the better. With the help of my old friend Sir Max Brown, whose promotion to full Permanent Secretary at the Department of Trade was the most welcome piece of news on that traumatic day, and of Mr Kenneth Clucas at Prices and Consumer Protection, the DTI was destroyed in twenty-four hours and in another twenty-four hours we had the three new departments in some kind of working order with the three Secretaries of State in place and all the staff allocated to their new commitments.

The key innovation which enabled this to happen at speed was the creation across all three departments common services – lawyers, economists, statisticians and, above all, finance and establishment staff – and 'common citizenship', which meant that we should be able to cross-post people between the three departments, as though the DTI still existed, and thus make the best use of the talent available. This arrangement proved acceptable to all concerned, from the staff side (the representatives of the unions) up to the Prime Minister.

We thought of these organisational devices as the immediate (and probably short-term) solution to an urgent problem. But as things turned out (except for the Department of Energy, which had opted for complete independence when it was created shortly before the general election of 1974 and provided one of my Second Permanent Secretaries, Jack Rampton, with a well-deserved promotion to Permanent Under-Secretary in the new department) the arrangements lasted until the DTI was re-created in 1983. Indeed, the same techniques were adopted when the Department of Transport was hived off from the Department of Environment in 1976, and are still operating. At the same time the Ministry of Posts and Telecommunications was broken up. Industry inherited one half: the Home Office the other. This change was also unplanned.

I went to meet Mr Benn in his office soon after breakfast. He was politeness itself and remained so during the whole of his time at the Department of Industry, though, as his *Diaries* for the period now show, he took an immediate personal dislike to me and arrived with a strong but completely false conviction that the department was the unquestioning ally of industrial management and had an ignorant bias against the trades unions and the 'workers' generally.

It was widely known that he had written the industrial chapter in the party manifesto with its proposals for a National Enterprise Board, planning agreements in the private sector, nationalisation of the ship-building and aircraft industries, a review of the plans for closing certain steel plants, and a heavy and varied load of work in connection with the Post Office. Above all, the main thrust was to bring about an irreversible shift of power in favour of the working classes. Not a light programme. The immediate embodiment of these hopes was to be an Industry Bill, which naturally involved a complete *volte-face* from the Tory approach.

To help Mr Benn in his work he had, on the political front, his Junior Ministers. He also imported Mrs Frances Morrell, a Labour activist, who later became known more widely as chairman of the Inner London Education Authority, and Francis Cripps, a brilliant young economist who was a party supporter. Some thought that this arrangement would be uncomfortable for all concerned, particularly as the Special Advisers had had no previous experience of working within the constraints of government and as the role of such people had not been closely defined. But owing to good sense all round there were no significant problems within the department. The only aspect of their activities that needed clarifying was the extent to which their responsibilities in Whitehall should restrain them from public comment on the work of the department.

Mr Benn was much taken with Mr Griffin's abilities and asked me if I would mind him inviting Ken to become one of his Special Advisers. I readily assented to this, but I thought the less of him for making without consultation with me an announcement that he had appointed Mr Griffin, who would 'also be available to advise the department' – not 'continue to be available'. The appointment was a success. It was particularly helpful to Mr Benn when he was trying to save the Triumph Motor Cycle business at Meriden and the *Scottish Daily News* at Glasgow from extinction by undertaking the novel and difficult task of forming viable 'workers' co-operatives'.

This was a characteristic initiative of Mr Benn's. Like many Ministers – and perhaps particularly Labour Ministers – he was disturbed when these two businesses showed clear signs of failure. He saw workers' co-operatives partly as a way of saving jobs and partly as a means of establishing two projects which would further the cause of workers' control which was such an important feature of his philosophy (though not that of the government). He had not, however, thought through the practical implications: for example, what should be the management structure, should everyone be paid the same, what about financial control, design and marketing?

His actual relations with workers were mixed. On the one hand he was said to be the only man in the country who could go into a roadside café and never be allowed to pay for his mugs of tea. On the other hand he did not have much experience of actual working conditions and relations in industry. Ken told me that at a meeting with the Meriden workers in their factory he once had to protect the Secretary of State from being manhandled by some of the workers.

Friend of the working class though he conceived himself to be, he was by no means always at one with the leaders of the TUC. At a meeting with Len Murray (he was surprised to hear that I was on first-name terms with Len) at Congress House, to which Ken Griffin and I accompanied him, he said apologetically that he was not yet quite ready with his proposals for 'industrial democracy'. 'Now we don't want any of that,' said Len, 'if we're going to have any of that, we'll do it from here.'

When Ken Griffin had done his stint at the DTI he was made deputy chairman of British Shipholders, where he did much useful work, especially in the sphere of industrial relations.

How to find a successor? Ken suggested Peter Turner of the TGWU. Discussions were proceeding well when someone told us that such a secondment was not permitted by the rules of that union. Whatever the precise impediment was, a message from me to Mr Jack Jones on a Friday resulted in the union's approval on the following Tuesday. Satisfactorily, Peter Turner was still in post when I retired in 1976.

In 1974 the department's most important job was to help Mr Benn to implement the proposals in the manifesto in so far as they were approved by the Prime Minister and the Cabinet as realistic in the circumstances in which the government took office. The Industry Bill was regarded as a high priority. To help with this Bill I formed a special team from some of the best talent available in the department. It is pleasing to report that the head of it (at Deputy Secretary level), who was Alan Lord, has since become the chief executive of Lloyd's. His second in command was Ron Dearing, who had started in a very junior job in the Civil Service and became in due course the chairman of the Post Office. The third was Peter Gregson, who rose via the Cabinet Office to be Permanent Secretary first of the Department of Energy and later of the DTI. They had strict instructions to do all they could to assist Mr Benn and to come to me if they encountered any serious difficulties from any quarter.

They naturally had some problems because they had a duty to draw attention to any proposals that seemed unlikely to make sense in practice. This is an occupational hazard for civil servants, as a critical view of an unrealistic proposal can seem to a Minister to be obstructive and be criticised accordingly – sometimes (though this is not supposed to happen) in public.

Of course the officials are not always right and this can lead to friction, which is to be avoided whenever possible. But sometimes they are right. In his witty book entitled *How to be a Minister*, which also contains some wise advice, Mr Gerald Kaufman remarked that during his whole time as Minister of State in the Department of Industry he never could discover what was supposed to go into a planning agreement.

Mr Benn himself liked dialectic, with or without an audience of Ministers or officials of the department. Sometimes meetings with him were rather like verbal boxing matches. Nothing new in that, as anyone who has worked with, say, Lord Hailsham or Denis Healey would testify. In Mr Benn's case the seating arrangements for his *tête-à-tête* several times a week with his Permanent Secretary emphasised his approach. Usually for such informal talks the Secretary of State and his Permanent Secretary would sit in armchairs in a corner of the office. Mr Benn wished us to face each other across the long narrow conference table next to his desk. As he did at meetings with deputations, he put a block of paper in front of him and drew a line down the middle. As the conversation proceeded, he noted my remarks to the left of the line and any comment or counter-argument of his to the right of the line. This did not make for a relaxed atmosphere and occasionally it was as though he were pointing a pistol at my head. Metaphorically, I would watch his finger tightening on the trigger and when I judged that he was about to fire I moved my head to one side. With any luck, I heard the bullet smack harmlessly into the woodwork behind me.

This was undeniably stimulating, but it was not a satisfactory way to conduct business in that it tended to suggest confrontation. However, the main task was to help him with his ambitious policies even though we were aware that by no means all of his ideas or proposals would be acceptable to the Prime Minister and his Cabinet colleagues. This applied particularly to any proposals that seemed likely to infringe the sovereignty of Parliament. So far as possible I tried to use as a yardstick the question: 'Does this proposal make practical sense and is it constitutional?'

It has been suggested that at some point the Prime Minister gave us guidance about the line to be taken with Mr Benn. This is quite untrue. At no time did we receive any such guidance. It was for me a rather lonely and stressful time, though I had the full support of my colleagues in and outside the department. The great thing was to keep the momentum of the work going without unnecessary explosions. This applied particularly to the Industry Bill. When the second reading of this Bill was approved in the Commons it was an important event for Mr Benn. He was warm in his congratulations to Alan Lord's team, and steady progress was made but the Bill was not passed into law until Mr Eric

Varley had succeeded Mr Benn as Secretary of State. Meanwhile Mr Benn faced two handicaps. The first was the general state of the economy. 1974 became the Year of Unanswered Questions. Could the existing international monetary system cope with the repercussions of the quadrupling of the price of oil? And if not, would the oil-consuming nations prove capable of agreeing on constructive modifications or would the pursuit of national self-interest lead to disarray? Would Britain remain a member of the EEC? Could a recession be prevented from developing into a slump? Could inflation be restrained from feeding upon itself and becoming hyper-inflation? Would clearer understanding of problems international and domestic lead to less divisive policies and practices? Would the strong at home and abroad appreciate that to take a short term selfish advantage could not merely sow the seeds of delay in recovery but even reap the whirlwind of disaster?

For a British industry recovering from a three-day week caused by a prolonged and determined miners' strike this was hardly a recipe for confidence. And the problems of the 'fringe banks', the insurance companies, the property market and the Stock Exchange did nothing to lighten the atmosphere. From March to September the political situation too was unsettled and, partly because of this, public understanding of the most serious economic crisis for many years was, to say the least, imperfect. Inflation was widely recognised as a serious threat to the economy – and even perhaps a danger to democratic ways and the fabric of society – but the recognition was muddled and partial, and it depended to a large degree on the extent to which individuals were affected by inflation. All in all it was an unsatisfactory time with an air of unreality about it. To some of us it seemed uncomfortably like the period of the 'phoney war' between September 1939 and the early summer of 1940.

The second handicap for Mr Benn was the factor much publicised since then by politicians: his increasing isolation in the Cabinet. But he did not resign, and the Prime Minister did not ask him to do so. In such a situation a Permanent Secretary is liable to be faced with a dilemma. To whom does his loyalty lie – his Secretary of State or the Prime Minister? To reply that his loyalty lies to the Crown, whose servant indeed he constitutionally is, does not provide a practical answer to the question. In my view his loyalty must lie to the former unless the Secretary of State is doing or contriving something that would be regarded by Parliament as improper. This would not of course absolve the Permanent Secretary from his duty as Accounting Officer. If the Permanent Secretary were to regard himself as primarily responsible to the Prime Minister as head of the government he would place himself in an untenable position *vis-à-vis* his Secretary of State who could object that he was not able to work with such a Permanent Secretary.

It also seemed to me important that I should not 'sneak' to senior colleagues outside the department about confidences from the Secretary of State. They were helpfully understanding about this.

This cannot be an easy line for a Permanent Secretary to follow, especially if, as would be almost inevitable, the press were to get out after him. This was the kind of situation in which rumours – and even false accusations – could all too easily arise and in which the confident confidential relationship that should exist between the Secretary of State and the Permanent Secretary would be hard to maintain. A prominent financial and economic journalist rang me to ask how many Accounting Officer minutes had been written to Mr Benn. Such a minute is unusual. It stems from the Permanent Secretary's responsibility to the Minister, the Treasury and the Public Accounts Committee of the House of Commons for proper and efficient administration of the funds voted to a department by Parliament. It is a very personal responsibility; he oversees the preparation of the department's annual estimates, signs the accounts and ensures that appropriate financial disciplines are established at all levels of the department.

Very occasionally a Secretary of State may propose a course of action that seems to the Permanent Secretary as Accounting Officer financially improper or irregular, perhaps in the sense of bypassing established procedures for scrutinising a novel proposal. In such a case, if persuasion fails, the Permanent Secretary has a duty to write to the Secretary of State what is colloquially called an Accounting Officer's minute, the existence of which must be reported to the Treasury, and, through the Comptroller and Auditor General, to the Public Accounts Committee. It is then up to the Secretary of State whether to proceed with his proposal as he is entitled to do.

All this takes time to emerge publicly. Meanwhile such issues are very sensitive. So I was not going to tell the journalist that between us Peter Carey and I had written to Mr Benn three Accounting Officer minutes. The journalist, whom I knew well, persisted with his enquiries for ten minutes or more but got no change. Mr Benn, who is free, as former Ministers often consider themselves to be, to comment on the situation has said publicly on one occasion I rang the editor of a national newspaper to be disloyal to him, but he never produced evidence to support this hostile assertion. Wherever the truth lies, my relationship with him was brought to an end for me in 1975 by a heart attack (mild happily, but unfortunately the harbinger of worse trouble four years later). When I returned to work after a few weeks' absence the Prime Minister was about to arrange for Mr Benn to move to the Department of Energy in a direct swap with Mr Eric Varley.

This was, I think, the twelfth time that a hospital had claimed me during my Civil Service career. Just as a Permanent Secretary described earlier in this narrative drew strength from the quotation from Benjamin Franklin I was much cheered when the astute Civil Service Medical Adviser, 'Tommy' Thomson, very much a Scot, wrote forecasting an early recovery and bringing to my attention four lines from a ballad about a fellow countryman of his:-

> Fight on, my men, said Sir Andrew Barton,
> For I am stricken but not slain.
> I'll lay me down and bleed awhile,
> And then I'll rise and fight again.

Fate had turned the kaleidoscope yet once more. Two years earlier the world had looked good from the DTI and there had been some talk of a move to one of three jobs in the public service, each of which would have been regarded as a promotion. For the

Foreign Office I decided not to throw my hat in the ring and I would probably not have got it anyway. For the Treasury which was offered to me, I did not consider myself fully enough qualified to make a really useful contribution in a single term of three years. For the Head of the Civil Service and Permanent Secretary of the Civil Service Department, in which my experience would have been the most relevant, I lost the contest to Sir Douglas Allen (later Lord Croham) then Permanent Secretary to the Treasury by what was described to me as 'in racing terms, a neck'.

So none of these prospects materialised, and in my remaining time in the service my tasks were to get as fit as possible, to see that Mr Varley was properly served and to leave everything as ship-shape as possible for my successor.

In the Civil Service the convention is that a retiring Permanent Secretary has no place in the process of nominating his successor to the Prime Minister. This is healthy because it lessens the likelihood of bias and eliminates a personal preference which would by definition be irrelevant to the future. There were, perhaps, four leading candidates, all of whom had considerable qualifications for the job. But in spite of the merits of the others I was pleased when the appointment of Peter Carey, whom I had increasingly encouraged to take the centre of the Civil Service stage at the Department of Industry, was approved by the Prime Minister.

The final year or so of a career lasting nearly forty years might seem to be a time for 'coasting home'. But for a Permanent Secretary there is no such thing as a quiet time. Chrysler (UK), the British Group of the Chrysler Corporation, had become inadequately competitive and its American parent threatened to liquidate it unless the government took it over. Would the government do so? Rescuing it would save 25,000 jobs (many in Scotland, where Chrysler's main factory was) and, it was suggested, as many others in the firms that supplied it. So there was a strong Scottish dimension to the problem and a strong employment dimension too. On the other hand, the firm's commercial prospects did not look too good, the rest of the British automotive industry would probably be advantaged if it were to close and a great deal of taxpayers' money would be required to help it get back into competitive shape, always assuming that management could be found to undertake the task successfully. There was no prospect of a take-over of Chrysler by another firm.

This was *par excellence* a case for skilled objective analysis by the Civil Service and a case for Ministers, in the light of that analysis, to decide how much weight to give to the strong political factors. These factors included the state of back-bench opinion in the House of Commons. There was much coming and going behind the scenes, including some tough discussions with the American parent company, in which Mr Harold Lever (later Lord Lever), Chancellor of the Duchy of Lancaster, with his experienced and ingenious financial mind, was known to have taken part.

The tussle continued into Cabinet and beyond. Resignations were narrowly avoided and it was Mr Varley's task as the Minister responsible for the automotive industry to announce the result in December 1975. Chrysler was to be rescued at a cost of over £100 million of the taxpayers' money and the Chrysler Corporation, not contributing any funds but sharing substantially in some of the guarantees, agreed to maintain their presence in the UK and to expand it to some extent. The facade of Cabinet unity was preserved and the Prime Minister agreed with my submission that if, as seemed certain, the Select Committee on Trade and Industry investigated the matter only one Minister (Mr Varley) should be allowed to appear.

The Chrysler struggle was the most dramatic that Mr Varley took part in. Although in earlier years he had been a member of Mr Harold Wilson's 'kitchen cabinet' he was not a great man for manoeuvre. The son of a miner, he had entered the mining industry in Derbyshire, worked his way up to be a member of the Area Executive Committee of the NUM and became a Member of Parliament in 1964. He married a local girl who did not care too much for London, and his family life was very important to him. Civil Servants do not always remember that a Minister lives and works in six different environments: his department, the Cabinet, Parliament, his Party, his constituency and his home. He has to adapt himself to each, and his occupational hazard is always to have too much to do. He can easily get swamped by the relentless volume of day-to-day work and not have enough time to think. One of the tasks of his senior Civil Servants – and of his Permanent Secretary in particular – is to help him to look beyond the immediate workload and to think about the wider context and the future.

The BBC came up with a proposal to make a TV profile of Mr Varley. The proposal was accepted and they turned out an agreeable programme that was sympathetic to him and revealed that his father was a 'natural' for television. In the days of the DTI, when Sir Geoffrey Howe was a Cabinet Minister as well as Mr Peter Walker, the BBC had been allowed to make a 'fly-on-the-wall' programme about Sir Geoffrey's work with officials in preparing a Bill on fair trading. This too was successful. Finally, around the time of my retirement, the BBC were allowed to arrange for Mr Vincent Hanna working on the 'Tonight' programme to do a substantial interview with the Permanent Secretary about his job.

Can the Civil Service get a square deal from the media? Some civil servants think not. They believe that it is better to keep heads below the parapet. This point of view seems to me wrong. The present climate of opinion is certainly adverse. The people most responsible for this are Ministers. But they more than anyone need a good Civil Service. This is not a matter for one political party. It should concern all those who hope to be members of future governments.

This is not to suggest that valid criticism should be withheld or that the Civil Service should be protected from economies in public expenditure, and energetic efforts should be made to root out any inefficiency or waste in order to get better value for money. But carrots are just as important as sticks and much depends on the underlying opinions of Ministers and on the public impression that they give of their attitudes. If these attitudes are critical they will be magnified by the media: as one experienced Director of Programmes said on Television: 'the world, so far as we are concerned, is about bad news.'

Ministers should be readier to speak up for the Civil Service in public, not least when there is widespread misunderstanding as there is, for example in the case of index-linked pensions.

Contrary to an impression that has been allowed to become widespread index-linking was introduced in the early 1970s with all-party support. Most people in the public sector have it and so do the employees of many major firms in the private sector. In pay negotiations the notional value of civil servants' contribution to a pension, had they made one, is deducted before any negotiations begin. Only one civil servant in five is paid above the national average and when anyone in the senior ranks of the DTI was approached by a business to transfer to the private sector (as several of them were) he or she was invariably offered more than twice their Civil Service salary.

The performance of Permanent Secretaries and others before Select Committees can influence informed opinion, but the wider public usually only gets the news of such meetings when there is a row. Retired senior civil servants can help a bit as several of us have had the chance to do, occasionally in solo 'slots' of up to thirty minutes on TV and radio and by articles in the press. On TV and Radio, the tricks of the trade need learning. For example: enquire beforehand who else is going to take part in the programme, ask whether it is to go out live or to consist of individual recordings edited by the producer, find out who the producer is and try to get assurances about the balance of the programme both in content and in time.

If something goes wrong, complaints machinery is available. But to use it effectively much persistence may be required. In 1981 a 'presenter' engaged by ATV broke his assurances to me that a programme mainly about the Civil Service would be balanced. I recorded with him an interview of forty minutes, of which three were devoted to industry and thirty seven to the Civil Service. When the programme was transmitted, not one of my remarks about the Civil Service was included, and criticism dominated the programme. The Complaints Review Board of the IBA upheld my complaint and after some three months of correspondence and telephone calls two 'firsts' were achieved. The IBA's ruling required Central Television, which by then held the Midlands franchise, to read out on the air a summary of the complaint, the verdict of the Complaints Review Board and an unqualified apology from the company. In addition the

IBA issued a press release about the complaint and the apology. They also undertook, as they were required to do, to publish the full report of the Complaints Review Board in their next annual report.

Although such apologies have their uses, prevention is better than cure, and it would be wrong to get too solemn about the whole thing. The serious question remains however: can the Civil Service and its friends do anything to change the present climate of opinion, especially in the media? In the orthodox type of confrontation programme on TV, (which is after all designed primarily for entertainment rather than enlightenment) one can on the whole only try to play a sound defensive game. With any luck the Civil Service spokesman, serving or retired, will appear not as the caricature of a bowler-hatted, pinstripe-suited stuffed shirt, but as a human being with interesting and constructive views and a manner enlivened by informality and good humour.

Better than those adversarial programmes was the Granada series 'State of the Nation' which attracted an audience of one million. In these hypothetical scenarios about controversial topics a number of former senior Civil Servants took part along with ex-Ministers, MPs, businessmen and others. The participants sat around the outside of a big horse-shoe shaped table while the 'Moderator' walked about the central space confronting any of the performers whom he chose with a question. Each person was nominated by the 'Moderator' to take a particular part, but you did not know which part or indeed anything much about the scenario except the title until the performance was underway. One programme related to freedom of information, a second to a nuclear power incident (years before Chernobyl) and a third to an industrial product which turned out to be defective and threatened to injure seriously the reputation of the manufacturer. There was also one about a revolution in an African country where Britain had important interests, and others on bribery and on taxation. This demonstration, limited – it is true – to the top ranks of the Service, made me think that this indirect approach had a more useful part to play than other techniques in helping the public to get a true picture of the Civil Service in operation.

In June 1976 my sixtieth birthday approached and the time had come to leave the Civil Service and start a second career. I took a last look at the view from my office. From the Ministry of Public Building and Works, with its headquarters in a rather unlovely building at the eastern end of Lambeth Bridge, I had enjoyed, aslant across the Thames, the impressive view of the Houses of Parliament that all the tourists stop outside Lambeth Palace to photograph. From Victoria Street one looked across Westminster School to the House of Lords. It seemed appropriate that during my eleven years as a Permanent Secretary I should have had constantly in view a physical reminder that Parliament stands at the centre of the stage.

CHAPTER SIX

From The Outside Looking In

Ten years spent as a non-executive director of half a dozen businesses after my retirement from Whitehall enabled me to see the Civil Service from a different point of view.

In 1976 a good number of people disapproved of retiring mandarins moving on to take 'lucrative' jobs in business. Greedy, unfair and open to abuse, it was suggested. Why could they not be content with their index-linked pensions? This view became increasingly out of date during a period when Whitehall was bringing in more and more businessmen into government and was itself being encouraged to send more and more people out to work in business for a couple of years or so. It also ignored the safeguards which existed, in particular the existence of the Diamond Committee, which had the job of vetting all applications to take up other employment within two years of retirement and of advising the Prime Minister whether the application should be approved, rejected or delayed.

However the media took up the running and a Select Committee of the House of Commons looked into the matter. After taking much evidence and indulging in some quite tough questioning, they were (in some cases I think reluctantly) convinced by the existing safeguards. They did not however think it right to adopt my proposal that anyone who had been in a contractual relationship with an outside firm should not be allowed to go straight into that firm on retirement. This to my mind was specially relevant to the Ministry of Defence where complicated contracts could not always be awarded after the submission of lump sum competitive tenders.

Since then the climate of public opinion has, I think, gradually changed during Mrs Thatcher's terms as Prime Minister. The deification of private enterprise coupled with denigration – or an approval of denigration – of the Civil Service has had the effect of making it more acceptable for civil servants, not only in mid-career but on retirement, to move out into the private sector. Indeed, a Secretary of State for Trade and Industry has been known to congratulate a girl who was leaving the Civil Service on 'joining the real world'.

Experience in the Civil Service is especially useful for work as a non-executive director. It enables the ex-civil servant to help his colleagues to take a strategic view because he looks at the company through a different pair of spectacles. And the need for non-executive directors of all kinds is steadily being more widely appreciated. However, knowing about Whitehall is not a good reason (except perhaps in Defence contracts) for appointing a civil servant as a director. I spent a minimal amount of time on this activity and made it a rule never to help represent a company's interests in negotiations with a government department.

A former civil servant, accustomed to take a wider view than an ordinary businessman has had a chance to do, should be able to contribute to a company's desire to become and to stay internationally competitive. This phrase has been the watchword of the DTI ever since 1970 when the department was first created. But other countries who started ahead of us are constantly advancing, and in many cases their leading firms have greater resources than ours do. So the competition becomes tougher all the time and I think that very few British firms can yet claim to be as internationally competitive as they need to be in order to survive effectively in the longer term.

Less than 2 per cent of all the companies in the UK account for 90 per cent of capital employed. To create and maintain conditions that will enable them to improve their profitability should therefore be the government's first concern. This does not necessarily mean giving them public money directly, though it may sometimes be in the national interest, for example, to help finance their R & D. It does however involve establishing a close relationship with them and being sufficiently informed to help to promote and defend their interests in international trade and expansion overseas.

The current politically fashionable encouragement of small firms is healthy if only because it generates a climate of enterprise, tends to increase net employment and because the most successful can ultimately grow to join their counterparts as the mainstays of the British industrial effort. But to highlight them as though they are the 'onlie begetters' of enterprise and employment is misguided. Suppose, for the sake of argument, that the policy is misguided, only a historian will be able to tell whether the Civil Service has done its job properly in that context, namely, to bring all the facts and considerations to the attention of Ministers, but if Ministers are determined upon their policy, to do all they can to support it.

Sitting in a government department and being capable of being in effective touch with so many aspects of industry it is easy to imagine that one's activities loom large in the minds of (at least) boards of directors. This is not so. Indeed one of one's earliest impressions on moving into industry is that apart from its macro-economic decisions and its close monitoring of, for example, the insurance industry the government is relatively unimportant to the business of strengthening balance sheets and keeping the profit and loss account in good shape. What is important is that when a government department does have to become involved, for example in export promotion or a proposed merger, it should be well enough informed to act intelligently and constructively and to have the necessary contacts at home and overseas to do so. This matters particularly when, as often happens, a government department has to work at considerable speed.

Where the Civil Service tends to be at its weakest is on major projects which involve more than one department. The preparations for Direct Broadcasting by Satellite (DBS) were a good case in point. Admittedly this is a very complicated, expensive and – above all – technologically demanding affair, affecting not only the UK but Europe and many other countries including the USA and Japan. In line with their belief in leaving the market free to make its own decisions the government limited their interest mainly to the technical transmission standard (the means by which the original image and sound are translated into electronic pulses, bounced off the satellite and returned to earth to be 'de-coded' into the sound and the picture, or more accurately the apparent picture, that reach the individual viewer). This intervention seemed necessary partly because it would not make practical sense either for broadcasting organisations or for manufacturers to have more than one standard in the UK and partly because the UK was a signatory to the agreement on standards in 1977 at the World Administrative Radio Conference for the Broadcasting Satellite Service (WARC) 77.

In 1982 the Home Secretary (Mr, later Viscount, Whitelaw) invited me to chair a small panel to assess the merits of rival transmission solutions favoured by the BBC (known as PAL) and the IBA (known as MAC). This was a fascinating exercise, greatly facilitated by Bernard Rogers, a very knowledgeable consultant with an international reputation. I got the impression that the Home Office were less than enthusiastic about the growing movement of opinion in the panel in favour of MAC, partly (I thought) because they were under the mistaken impression that everyone at the BBC was opposed to it. We corrected this impression at our meeting with the Home Secretary to present our report. At the end of the meeting he accepted our recommendations unreservedly, taking into account the much greater potential for future technical development inherent in MAC.

The next stage, in which I had not expected to be involved, was to persuade the Europeans to adopt MAC. This was by no means easy, especially because the Germans were slow to be convinced and the French had their own ideas. But success was eventually achieved though after I had withdrawn from the project in frustration at the lack of purposefulness and co-operation between the Home Office, the DTI and the FCO. The Prime Minister refused to accept the evidence of these shortcomings which I presented to her and declined to adopt my suggestion that a senior Minister should be charged with ensuring effective co-ordination of the government's interests in the subject.

Meanwhile an EEC directive was agreed embodying the essential elements of the MAC standards. But as time went by difficulties emerged about the design of the semi-conductors needed to decode the signals transmitted by the MAC technique. Meanwhile Sky Television, a company chaired by Mr Rupert Murdoch, opted for a lower-powered, less sophisticated system related to PAL, which was more easily compatible with existing receivers. As it was using a waveband not allocated to a European country by WARC77, and was not covered by the EEC directive, it did not have to use MAC.

Against this, a consortium called British Satellite Broadcasting had won a contract to run three of the five UK DBS channels using the MAC transmission system. So, as things turned out, though much was achieved, the original proposal for which my panel was set up was nullified. A wry conclusion to a stimulating assignment.

What about Mrs Thatcher and the Civil Service? When she first came into office there was the usual expectation that the size of the Service would be reduced. For many years, Tory governments, some more successfully than others, aimed to get rid of many of the controls and incentives which their Labour predecessors had put in place, and to have much less central planning. Over the years the Civil Service became used to growing in size after the arrival of a Labour government and contracting when the Tories returned to power.

But with Mrs Thatcher's arrival two new factors were introduced. The first arose from her determination to change the whole climate of opinion in the country in the direction of private enterprise and a market economy. This applied particularly to financial and economic matters in which she and her mentors from the private sector were more sure-footed. She determined to 'move the goalposts' and get the country clean away from the almost automatically alternating policies of previous governments, none of whom had proved able (once the spirit of unity generated by the Second World War had evaporated) to establish a lasting climate of success.

In this sense she was – and is – translating a philosophy into a revolution, and revolutions are no time for delicate negotiations or for pussy-footing around. It is as though she had drawn her approach from a German military textbook. Establish the *Schwerpunkt* (the main thrust). Do not disperse your efforts. Do not worry if there are some untidinesses on the flanks: you can always clear them up afterwards. This approach is fine so long as you and your supporters have done the necessary homework (which has been noticeably lacking in almost all areas of social policy). This drive required that she have a Cabinet of very much like-minded Ministers. It also required that she should have Permanent Secretaries and other mandarins whom she regarded as not only receptive to her policies (which tradition required them to be) but who would have the drive and enthusiasm to get them implemented effectively and at speed. She therefore took a distinctly closer interest in top appointments in the Civil Service than most of her predecessors had done. She was determined that anyone who filled a top post should be 'one of us'.

This approach clearly had merits in the circumstances but it also had some destabilising effects. These effects were not too serious in themselves. They were however food and drink to the media ('Shake-up in Whitehall' and so on) but they became destructive when they were linked, as they were, to public denigration by Ministers of the Service as a whole. This set rolling a bandwagon onto which a good many Tory back-benchers (many of them new to Westminster and Whitehall) readily jumped. Ironically the extremely successful TV programmes 'Yes, Minister' and 'Yes, Prime Minister', hilarious though they were, also played their part in persuading the public that Sir Humphrey and his colleagues were true to life. All this did not matter so much to the mandarins who were used to such pressures. Some, it is true, were unhappy about manifestations of the 'My Prime Minister right or wrong' syndrome, and some – on occasion – felt that it would be a waste of time to produce statistics or advice which might tend to point in a different direction from Ministers' ideas.

As mentioned earlier in this book, in home affairs the Treasury always had a tendency to centralise too much – to the detriment of efficiency and in disregard of the constitutional responsibilities of individual departments. Under Mrs Thatcher this tendency has increased and is not limited to Whitehall. Though the government is rightly critical of a few local authorities this centralisation extends to relations with local authorities as a whole and thus risks emasculating a crucial tier of influence in British democracy. This tendency also has its dangers within the Civil Service. Very few Treasury officials have any substantial experience outside that department and many have none at all. Highly intelligent though they are, reasoning and imagination are no substitute for experience. Because of the nature of their jobs Treasury officials are less accustomed to 'getting out on the ground' than those of almost any other department. This, coupled with the impact of increased centralisation, is unhealthy and could prove dangerous.

It is perhaps more defensible in macro-economic matters, though even there it took a long time to persuade the Chancellor of the defects of the Friedman version of a monetarist policy. But this approach is more dangerous when it is applied to issues on which the Chancellor and his officials are less well informed and is likely to prove more damaging. This has already been the case in social fields such as education, the health service, prisons, and inner cities where policy has often not been grounded in considered advice. This difficulty is compounded by the government's unwillingness to appoint any committees that do not consist of 'true believers'. Some mandarins respond better than others to this régime. All are change-makers for that has been the central feature of their careers. But some – particularly those who are by nature and experience regulators rather than doers – have been slow to accommodate themselves to the revolution, and their prospects have suffered accordingly.

The natural tendency of many of Mrs Thatcher's Ministers is to laud the virtue of business methods. To someone who has worked in both the public and the private sectors this is not necessarily a recommendation! In any case business has the ultimate imperative of balance sheets and profit and loss accounts while a government's job is to provide the progressive framework within which the prime movers can do their best work.

Mrs Thatcher's changes did one particularly useful thing. They highlighted the importance of management in government departments and put it up alongside the formation of policy as a top priority. It would be specially important that the Permanent Secretaries of the future should be as capable at the first as they traditionally have been at the second. This development would also have its effect lower down in departments. This would clearly impinge on the promotion prospects of particular people however much trouble was taken over training. The appointment at the centre of government as efficiency adviser of Sir Robin Ibbs, formerly of ICI, emphasised the importance of that work and carried usefully forward the efficiency scrutinies initiated in the 1970s by Mr Derek (later Lord) Rayner, seconded from Marks & Spencer.

The strengthening of the regional offices, announced in 1988 and inspired no doubt partly by the high cost of office space and housing in Greater London, was a constructive idea even if it implied a greater degree of intervention on the part of government than the Conservative Party's philosophy seemed to comprehend. It would also throw the recruitment net usefully wider. Plans were too announced to increase the dispersal of whole government activities to the regions. This was a continuation of such moves as the dispersal in the 1970s of the Business Statistics Office to Newport and the Companies Registration Office to Cardiff. (Indeed one of Mr Wilson's governments actually got so far as to announce that the Government Chemists Department was to be moved from London to Cumbria. Mercifully common sense ultimately prevailed over political expediency.)

But any idea that the ultimate aim should be to move all the 'executive' functions of government out of London, leaving a small corps of policy-makers behind, is unrealistic. To take only three examples: the Export Credits Guarantee Department needs to be near the City, and the Treasury will fight to the death to keep the headquarters of the Inland Revenue and the Customs and Excise in London.

There emerged from Sir Robin Ibbs' stable a report by three junior members of the Cabinet Office putting forward a superficial proposal that most executive functions should be transmuted into 'agencies' with more or less unfettered freedom of action including delegated powers to recruit staff from outside the Service for shorter or longer periods. The government rightly took the view that in any decision with political implications, for example a proposal to increase significantly the cost of a driving licence, Ministerial approval would still be required. They also coralled the chief executive's independence by proposing to make not him but the Permanent Secretary of the department concerned the Accounting Office to the Public Accounts Committee. But later they changed their minds about this.

It is certainly healthy that those responsible for more or less self-contained executive functions should be given greater delegated powers than has been traditional in many cases. It is also a good idea to introduce targets of achievement wherever this makes practical sense. But to propose, as has been done, that the Royal Parks should be run on a commercial basis would risk ruining them as the national assets that they at present are.

The introduction of business methods when they are relevant and the constant search for greater efficiency should be unrelenting. But I think it fundamentally important that the Civil Service should remain a 'service'. It is the consciousness of this that binds the whole show together, necessarily not quite to the same extent as in the armed services, but in very much the same way. It is a matter of pride for civil servants that they are in the service of the Crown. This sense of service is critically important to their continuing integrity and to their ability to meet, day in and day out, the often complex and challenging demands of the government of the day, Parliament and the public.

Index